Jane Austen

HELEN AMY

AMBERLEY

First published in 2013

Amberley Publishing
The Hill, Stroud
Gloucestershire, GL5 4EP

www.amberley-books.com

© Helen Amy 2013

The right of Helen Amy to be identified as
the Author of this work has been asserted in
accordance with the Copyrights, Designs and
Patents Act 1988.

ISBN 978 1 4456 0586 9 hardback
ISBN 978 1 4456 1573 8 ebook

British Library Cataloguing in Publication Data.
A catalogue record for this book is available
from the British Library.

Typeset in 11pt on 16pt Palatino.
Typesetting and Origination by Amberley Publishing
Printed in the UK.

CONTENTS

INTRODUCTION

Jane Austen, the seventh child of an English country parson, was brought up in north Hampshire in the late Georgian period. Jane was born into a hierarchical society in which everyone knew their place. It was also a patriarchal society, in which most women were dependent, second-class citizens who were expected to devote their lives to being good wives, housekeepers and mothers.

Jane lived during a time of great upheaval, when England was changing rapidly. The old order was being challenged in a number of ways. The country was turning from an agricultural into an industrial nation. A new class of men were emerging, their money coming from trade and industry. This new money was replacing the old inherited wealth. A new meritocratic system was replacing the old patronage, and Anglicanism was being challenged by Methodism. There were also stirrings of political discontent, inspired by the French Revolution, and serious social and industrial unrest. Jane was not directly affected by many of these changes, as life in peaceful, rural north Hampshire continued in much the same way as it had done for centuries. However, this changing order formed the backdrop to Jane's life as well as her novels.

Jane belonged to a happy and loving family, whose members were clever, intellectual, talented and cultured. In an age when the standard female education was very limited, Jane was fortunate enough to receive an excellent education from her father, an experienced tutor of boys. She also improved herself by reading widely. Jane, therefore, had the right cultural and educational background to enable her considerable natural talents to thrive.

Jane wrote from an early age, both for pleasure, and to entertain and to amuse her family and friends. By the age of twenty she had written her first full-length novel. In her novels Jane wrote about life in late Georgian England from the point of view of a woman. She kept her writing a secret from all but a few people, and even when her novels were published Jane refused to be named as their author. Jane's genius as a novelist was not recognised during her lifetime; her fame grew slowly after her early death at the age of forty-one, until she reached a worldwide readership and cult status as an author.

This book tells Jane's story, as far as possible in the words of people who knew her, to many of whom she was, first and foremost, a much-loved family member. The biographies of later generations of Jane's family, who had access to family papers and memories, are also used, as are Jane's own letters.

1

CHILDHOOD
1775–1786

On 16 December 1775 Cassandra Austen, wife of the Reverend George Austen, gave birth to her seventh child at the rectory in Steventon, Hampshire. The next day George Austen wrote to his sister-in-law, Susannah Walter, announcing the birth.

> Steventon, December 17th 1775
>
> Dear Sister,
>
> You have doubtless been for some time in expectation of hearing from Hampshire, and perhaps wondered a little we were in our old age grown such bad reckoners, but so it was, for Cassy certainly expected to have been brought to bed a month ago; however, last night the time came, and without a great deal of warning, everything was soon happily over. We have now another girl, a present plaything for her sister Cassy, and a future companion. She is to be Jenny, and seems to be as if she would be as like Harry as Cassy is to Neddy. Your sister, thank God, is pure well after it.[1]

Although known as Jenny throughout her childhood, the new baby was christened Jane, as her father recorded in the family Bible: 'Born 16 Decr 1775. Privately baptised 17 Decr 1775. Rec'd into the church

5 Apl 1776. Sponsors Revd. Mr. Cooke Rector of Bookham, Surry. Mrs. Jane Austen of Sevenoaks, Kent, Father's uncle's wife. Mrs. Musgrave of Chinnor, Oxon.'

George Austen's forebears came from the Tenterden and Sevenoaks area of Kent. One branch of his family had been wealthy clothiers and landowners, but the branch from which George descended was not well off. George was born in 1731 to William Austen and his wife Rebecca, who already had a son from her first marriage. William was a surgeon, which was a lowly profession at that time. By the age of nine George had lost both parents, and he and his sisters Philadelphia and Leonora were taken in and provided for by their wealthy uncle Francis, a successful lawyer in Tonbridge, with a large family of his own.

George attended Tonbridge School and won an open scholarship to St John's College, Oxford, which he entered at the age of sixteen. After graduating with a Master of Arts degree in 1754, George was ordained as a deacon and then a priest. He was appointed perpetual curate of Shipbourne in Kent, and also worked for a time as a master at his old school. George later returned to St John's College, where he was assistant college chaplain and junior proctor for the year 1759–60. In the latter position he was responsible for enforcing university regulations and, because of his good looks, particularly his bright hazel eyes and wavy hair, George became known as 'the handsome proctor'. In 1760 George added to his achievements by obtaining a Bachelor of Divinity degree. Four years later he married Miss Cassandra Leigh at Walcot church in Bath.

Cassandra was from a higher social class than her husband, having been born in 1737 into an ancient illustrious family. One of her ancestors was Sir Thomas Leigh, a Lord Mayor of London during the reign of Elizabeth I. Cassandra was very proud to be related to the Leighs of Stoneleigh Abbey in Warwickshire. Her father, a former fellow of All Souls College, Oxford, was the vicar of Harpsden in Oxfordshire and her uncle, Sir Theophilus Leigh, was Master of Balliol College. It was probably at this uncle's home that Cassandra first met her future husband.

After their marriage the Austens set up home in Deane, Hampshire and George became rector of the neighbouring village of Steventon. This living was given to him by a wealthy distant cousin, Thomas Knight of Godmersham in Kent, who owned extensive land and property in Kent and Hampshire. The Austens were a well-suited couple and their marriage was a happy and successful one. The sensible, well-educated, clever and witty Cassandra was an excellent wife for the gentle, placid, cheerful, scholarly and amiable George. As the daughter of a country clergyman, she was well prepared for her role as a rector's wife in rural Hampshire. Mrs Austen's widowed mother and her seven-year-old ward George Hastings shared the Austens' first marital home. George, the son of Warren Hastings, later the Governor General of Bengal, had been sent home to be educated and was being cared for by the Leigh family. Little George died of diphtheria in the autumn of 1764, to the great distress of Mrs Austen.

It was not long, however, before the Austens had a family of their own. Their first three sons, James, George and Edward, were born at Deane in 1765, 1766 and 1767 respectively. In the summer of 1771 the family moved to Steventon Rectory. This event was recorded in the following description by James's son James-Edward Austen-Leigh, known to the family as Edward, in *A Memoir of Jane Austen and Other Family Recollections* published in 1869: 'The lane between Deane and Steventon has long been as smooth as the best turnpike road; but when the family removed from the one residence to the other in 1771, it was a mere cart track, so cut up by deep ruts as to be impassable for a light carriage. Mrs Austen, who was not then in strong health, performed the short journey on a feather-bed, placed upon some soft articles of furniture in the waggon which held their household goods.'[2]

The remaining Austen children were born at Steventon Rectory; Henry in 1771, Cassandra in 1773, Francis, known as Frank, in 1774, Jane in 1775 and Charles in 1779. All the children were sent, as soon as they were weaned, to be cared for by a woman who lived in Deane, possibly Elizabeth, wife of John Littleworth, who was known locally as Nanny Littlewart. This practice was described by Jane's nephew.

> Her (Jane's) mother followed a custom, not unusual in those days, though it seems strange to us, of putting out her babies to be nursed in a cottage in the village. The infant was daily visited by one or both of its parents, and frequently brought to them at the parsonage, but the cottage was its home, and must have remained so till it was old enough to run about and talk; for I know that one of them, in after-life, used to speak of his foster mother as 'Movie', the name by which he had called her in his infancy … It would certainly seem from the results that it was a wholesome and invigorating system…[3]

Mrs Austen's affection for – and pride in – her children is evident in letters she wrote to her sister-in-law Susannah Walter. In November 1772 she wrote, 'My little boy (Henry) is come home from nurse, and a fine, stout little fellow he is, and can run anywhere, so now I have all four at home, and some time in January I expect a fifth…'[4] In June 1773 she wrote of her daughter Cassandra: 'I suckled my little girl thro' the first quarter; she has been weaned and settled at a good woman's at Deane just eight weeks; she is very healthy and lively, and puts on her short petticoats today.'[5] Another letter, written when Mrs Austen was expecting Jane, contained more details of her young family.

> We are all, I thank God, in good health, and I am more nimble and active than was last time, expect to be confined some time in

November. My last boy is very stout, and has run alone these two months, and is not yet sixteen months old. My little girl talks all day long, and in my opinion is a very entertaining companion. Henry has been in breeches some months, and thinks himself near as good a man as his brother Neddy. Indeed no one would judge by their looks that there was above three years and a half difference in their ages, one is so little and the other so great.[6]

In 1773 George Austen's uncle Francis bought him the living of Deane. He supported his family with the stipends from both livings, in addition to the income and produce from the farmland which went with Steventon Rectory. The family retained the produce of the garden and the dairy for their own use. Although better off than most clergymen of the time, George Austen's income was not enough to support his growing family. He, therefore, began to teach a few sons of the local aristocracy and gentry. These boys were taught alongside George's own sons, whom he tutored from a young age to prepare them for university. The pupils boarded at the rectory and were looked after by Mrs Austen. In 1779, when Jane was four, her eldest brother James completed his education at home and went to his father's old college at Oxford. He was awarded a Founder's Kin scholarship because an ancestor of his mother was related to the founder of the college.

While the Austen boys received a typical male education in the classics and enjoyed outdoor pursuits, such as riding and shooting, their sisters spent most of their time with their mother. From a young age, Jane and her sister became familiar with the role most girls of their class were expected to assume in adulthood – that of wife, mother and housekeeper. They accompanied their mother as she brewed, baked, gardened, tended to the family's cows and chickens, supervised the servants, and looked after the needs of all members of the household.

Life in the Austen home was happy, cheerful and harmonious, providing Jane with the best possible start in life. Her contentment came from belonging to a well-educated, intellectual and cultivated family whose members were close, loving and united. Her nephew described the affection and unity within the family in his *Memoir*. 'The family talk had abundance of spirit and vivacity, and was never troubled by disagreements even in little matters, for it was not their habit to dispute or argue with each other: above all, there was strong family affection and firm union, never to be broken but by death.[7] It cannot be doubted that her early years were bright and happy, living, as she did, with indulgent parents, in a cheerful home, not without agreeable variety of society.'[8]

Jane was affectionate towards all her brothers, but her mother noticed her particular closeness to Henry, whom she resembled both physically and temperamentally. They shared a cheerful, positive and optimistic outlook on life. Jane's niece Caroline described Henry as 'her especial pride and delight', but added that 'of all her family, the nearest and dearest throughout her whole life was, undoubtedly, her sister'.[9] She considered the love and closeness between Jane and Cassandra to be 'the most perfect affection and confidence'.[10] Jane adored her sister from early childhood and could not bear to be separated from her, causing her mother to remark on one occasion that 'if Cassandra were going to have her head cut off, Jane would insist on sharing her fate'.[11] Cassandra, being two years older, was the leader in the relationship, and Jane looked up to her sister throughout her life, regarding her as 'wiser and better than herself'.[12]

The Austen family enjoyed spending time together and often read aloud to each other in the evenings. They also enjoyed performing plays together each Christmas and summer. These amateur productions, which began in 1782, were performed to an audience of family and friends in the dining room, or in a barn across the road from the rectory. The younger children and

George Austen's pupils joined in with these performances. The plays performed were mostly popular comedies of the time, with an additional prologue and epilogue written by James. Jane's memories of her family's love of acting later inspired an important part of the plot of her novel *Mansfield Park*.

Another pastime enjoyed by the family was the writing and reading of charades and conundrums. In *Personal Aspects of Jane Austen*, Mary Augusta Austen-Leigh imagined Jane 'as one of a family group gathered round the fireside … to enliven the long evenings of a hundred years ago by merry verses and happy, careless inventions of the moment, such as flowed without difficulty from the lively minds and ready pens of those amongst whom she lived'.[13] Later Jane contributed charades and verses of her own to this family entertainment.

The Austens kept in contact with a number of relatives by letter and exchanged visits with them. On the Austen side of the family were the Hancocks and Walters. George's sister Philadelphia was married to a surgeon named Tysoe Saul Hancock, who worked for the East India Company, and spent her early married life in India. They had one daughter, Eliza, who was born in 1761. William Hampson Walter was George's elder half-brother, who lived with his wife Susannah and their family in Kent. On the Leigh side of the family were Mrs Austen's brother James Leigh-Perrot and his wife Jane who lived in Berkshire, and also had a home in Bath. Mrs Austen was close to her sister Jane, wife of Edward Cooper, an Anglican clergyman, who had homes in Southcote, near Reading, and in Bath. The Coopers had two children, Edward born in 1770, and Jane born in 1771. It is likely that Jane Austen acquired her early knowledge of Bath during visits paid to the Coopers there. The Austens also kept in touch with Jane's godfather Samuel Cooke, rector of Bookham in Surrey, whose wife Cassandra was Mrs Austen's cousin, and their three children Theophilus, Mary and George.

Another reason for Jane's childhood contentment was her attachment to the rectory in which she grew up. Her nephew Edward recorded his memories of her childhood home.

The house itself stood in a shallow valley, surrounded by sloping meadows, well sprinkled with elm trees, at the end of a small village of cottages, each well provided with a garden, scattered about prettily on either side of the road. It was sufficiently commodious to hold pupils in addition to a growing family, and was in those times considered to be above the average of parsonages; but the rooms were furnished with less elegance than would now be found in the most ordinary dwellings. No cornice marked the junction of wall and ceiling; while the beams which supported the upper floors projected into the rooms below in all their naked simplicity, covered only by a coat of paint or whitewash…[14]

North of the house, the road from Deane to Popham Lane ran at a sufficient distance from the front to allow a carriage drive, through turf and trees. On the south side the ground rose gently, and was occupied by one of those old-fashioned gardens in which vegetables and flowers are combined, flanked and protected on the east by one of the thatched mud walls common in that country, and overshadowed by fine elms. Along the upper or southern side of this garden, ran a terrace of the finest turf…[15]

Edward's half-sister Anna also remembered the rectory garden.

On the sunny side was a shrubbery and flower garden, with a terrace walk of turf which communicated by a small gate with what was termed 'the wood walk', a path winding through clumps of underwood and overhung by tall elm trees, skirting the upper side of the home meadows. The lower bow window, which looked so cheerfully into the sunny garden and up the middle grass walk bordered with strawberries, to the sundial at the end, was that of my grandfather's study, his own exclusive property, safe from the bustle of all household cares.[16]

Jane also loved the village of Steventon and the countryside surrounding her home. Edward Austen-Leigh described Steventon as

> a small rural village upon the chalk hills of north Hants, situated in a winding valley about seven miles from Basingstoke … It is certainly not a picturesque country; it presents no grand or extensive views; but the features are small rather than plain. The surface continuously swells and sinks, but the hills are not bold, nor the valleys deep; and though it is sufficiently well-clothed with woods and hedgerows, yet the poverty of the soil in most places prevents the timber from attaining a large size. Still it has its beauties. The lanes wind along in a natural curve, continually fringed with irregular borders of native turf, and lead to pleasant nooks and corners … Of this somewhat tame country, Steventon, from the fall of the ground, and the abundance of its timber, is certainly one of the prettiest spots.[17]

Edward considered that the most beautiful feature of Steventon was its hedgerows. 'A hedgerow, in that country, does not mean a thin formal line of quickset, but an irregular border of copse-wood and timber, often wide enough to contain within it a winding footpath, or a rough cart track. Under its shelter the earliest primroses, anemones, and wild hyacinths were to be found; sometimes, the first bird's-nest; and, now and then, the unwelcome adder.'[18]

Jane's nephew believed that 'the real foundations of her fame were laid in Steventon' and considered the surrounding countryside to be 'the cradle of her genius. These were the first objects which inspired her young heart with a sense of the beauties of nature. In strolls along those wood-walks, thick-coming fancies rose in her mind, and gradually assumed the forms in which they came forth to the world.'[19]

The other important buildings in Steventon, apart from the rectory, were the church where George Austen was rector, and the manor house. These buildings were situated, close together, in a secluded place away from the brick-and-flint cottages of the village. The small twelfth-century church of St Nicholas, with its tower and short-needled spire, was surrounded by a graveyard overshadowed by an ancient yew tree. Constance Hill, the author of *Jane Austen, Her Home and Her Friends*, published in 1901, wrote the following description of the route from the rectory to the church:

> We are told that a path called the 'Church walk' started from the eastern end of the terrace and ascended the steep hill behind the parsonage to the church ... Let us cross the meadow, gentle reader, where the path ran which the Austens must have trod each Sunday morning as they walked to church. Leaving the meadow, we enter a small wood, and, on emerging from this wood, find ourselves on high tableland. There above us stands the church, a modest edifice of sober grey, seen through a screen of great arching elms and sycamore. Behind us stretches a fertile valley fading into a blue distance.[20]

Just behind the church was a wicket gate which led straight onto the lawn of Steventon manor house, with its mullioned windows and tall chimneys, built in the reign of Henry VIII. The manor house belonged to Thomas Knight, George Austen's distant cousin who had presented him with the livings of Steventon, but was rented to the Digweed family during the eighteenth century.

The Austen family's social circle included the type of large landowners and lesser gentry who later featured in Jane's novels. The former included Lord Dorchester of Kempshott Park, Lord Bolton of Hackwood Park, both near Basingstoke, and Lord Portsmouth of Hurstbourne, five miles east of Andover. Lord Portsmouth's son Lord Lymington was a pupil of George Austen for a short time, and his family remained in touch with the Austens. Also in this social circle was the family of William Chute, who owned The Vyne, a grand country house of Tudor origins near Basingstoke, and was Master of the Vyne Hunt. Chute, who was the Tory MP for Hampshire, was described in the following words by Edward Austen-Leigh:

> He had a fair round face with a most agreeable countenance expressive of good humour and intelligence … I can fancy that I see him, trotting up to the meet at Freefolk Wood, or St John's, sitting rather loose on his horse, and his clothes rather loose upon him – the scarlet coat flapping open, a little whitened at the collar by the contact of his hair powder and the friction of his pigtail; the frill of his shirt above, and his gold watch-chain and seal below, both rather prominent, the short knee-breeches scarcely meeting the boot-tops.[21]

Other landed proprietors known to the Austens included the Bigg-Wither family of Manydown House, near Deane, and the families of Henry Portal of Laverstoke House, near Hurstbourne, and his brother John of nearby Freefolk Priors. The lesser gentry in the Austens' social circle included the Digweeds, whose four sons were of a similar age to the Austen children, the Harwoods, and the Terrys who lived in the manor houses of Steventon, Deane and the nearby village of Dummer respectively. The Austens' closest friends were the Reverend George Lefroy, the rector of Ashe, and his wife Anne and Mrs Lloyd, a clergyman's widow, and her daughters Mary and Martha who lived in the parsonage at Deane. The Lloyd sisters became close friends of Jane and Cassandra, and eventually married into the Austen family. The world in which the Austens moved was comprised of such neighbours and friends, as well as their relations on both sides of the family.

Although by no means as well off as the local gentry, the Austens were accepted on equal terms with them. This was because George Austen was an educated, professional man with an important position in the local community, and because he was a relative of Thomas Knight, who owned most of the surrounding land and property. Edward Austen-Leigh noted that

> their situation had some peculiar advantages beyond those of ordinary rectories. Steventon was a family living. Mr Knight, the patron, was also proprietor of nearly the whole parish. He never resided there, and consequently the rector and his children came to be regarded in the neighbourhood as a kind of representatives of the family. They shared with the principal tenant the command of an excellent manor, and enjoyed, in this reflected way, some of the consideration usually awarded to landed proprietors.[22]

Further down the social scale the Austen family came into regular contact with the members of the labouring class, who lived in the cottages of Steventon and Deane, as George Austen had pastoral responsibility for them. His wife was also involved in helping her husband's poor parishioners.

Only one shadow darkened the happiness of Jane's early years. Her second-eldest brother, George, suffered from epilepsy and learning disabilities and was probably deaf as well; for this reason he did not live with his family. The Austens made financial provision for George and visited him at the home of the family who looked after him in the nearby village of Monk Sherborne, but he was not really part of their lives. Apart from a few early letters which mention George and reveal his parents' concern for him, he was not mentioned in later correspondence or any family memoirs.

Jane was probably taught to read and write by her mother. It was customary in the eighteenth century for mothers of the Austen family's social class to provide their children, of both sexes, with their earliest education, including moral and spiritual instruction. Then in the spring of 1783, at a very tender age, Jane went to Oxford with her sister and her cousin Jane Cooper, to be tutored by

Mrs Ann Cawley. Mrs Cawley was Jane Cooper's aunt, being the sister of her father Edward Cooper. It is thought that Mrs Austen was more in favour of sending the girls away to be educated than their father was. It must have eased her heavy domestic workload and made life more comfortable in the overcrowded rectory. This event was described by Mary Augusta Austen-Leigh in *Personal Aspects of Jane Austen*. (Miss Austen-Leigh gave an earlier date for this than the generally accepted one.)

> Space was probably needed within their own home for the reception of George Austen's pupils, and his little daughters, at the ages of nine and six, were sent to be educated elsewhere, not, as we are told, because it was supposed that Jane at six years old required very much education, but because it would have broken her heart to be separated from Cassandra. The sisters, therefore, went together to Oxford, there to be placed under the care of Mrs Cawley, who was a connection of their mother and the widow of a Principal of Brasenose College; a lady of whom no record remains beyond the fact that she was a stiff-mannered person. Mrs Cawley removed after a short time to Southampton, and by so doing very nearly put an end to Jane's short existence, for in that town both she and Cassandra fell very ill of what was then called putrid fever and Jane's life was at the time despaired of. Mrs Cawley would not at first write word of this illness to Steventon Rectory, but Jane Cooper, the little girls' cousin, who was one of the party, thought it right to do so, an action which was probably instrumental in saving the life of Jane. Mrs Austen at once set off for Southampton together with her sister, Mrs Cooper, and they brought with them a remedy, to the use of which Jane's recovery was ascribed.[23]

Under their mother's care the Austen sisters recovered but, tragically, Mrs Cooper had caught the infection and died at her home in Bath as a result. The girls did not return to Southampton after their recovery.

In the year 1783 Jane's brother Edward was adopted. Thomas Knight, the son of Thomas Knight the wealthy kinsman who had presented George Austen with the living of Steventon, was in need of an heir as he and his wife Catherine were childless. The Knights had grown fond of the placid, easy-going and likeable Edward Austen, who often stayed at their home in Godmersham in Kent. Eventually the Knights asked George Austen if they could adopt Edward and make him their heir. Mr Austen was reluctant to agree initially, as he was preparing his son for university, and was worried about the disruption to his education. The practical and sensible Mrs Austen, however, realising that Edward was less academic than his brothers, could see what an excellent opportunity was being offered to him and urged her husband to agree. At the age of sixteen, therefore, Edward Austen was formally adopted by the Knights. This event was recorded in a silhouette picture by the London artist William Wellings showing George Austen handing over his son to Thomas Knight. Edward became heir to the Knights' vast estates in Kent and Hampshire, and agreed to adopt their name when he came into his inheritance. Jane was only eight at the time of her brother's adoption and move to Kent. This event became more significant to her as she grew older. Edward remained in close contact with his birth family and they visited him regularly. These visits opened up a whole new area of experience for Jane, which she later put to good use in her novels.

From 1783 to 1785 Jane and Cassandra were presumably tutored at home. It is known that Jane studied the rudiments of French grammar, because a French primer, inscribed with her name and the date of 5 December 1783, is still in the possession of the Austen family. Then in the spring of 1785 the Austen sisters left home again to join their cousin Jane at boarding school.

It was a common practice in eighteenth-century England for members of the professional and gentry classes to send their daughters to boarding school. The education provided at these schools placed great emphasis on the acquisition of good manners, social graces and ladylike accomplishments such as drawing, sewing, dancing and singing. Academic learning was positively discouraged in girls, as it was considered unwomanly, and it was believed that females were intellectually incapable of serious study. The standard education for girls was designed to attract suitors and prepare them for lives focused on husband, home and family. Another purpose of this education was to enable girls to entertain at social functions, and help them to fill the many leisure hours at their disposal.

Jane Austen portrayed the education provided at late eighteenth-century boarding schools in her novel *Emma*; she no doubt drew on her own experience when she imagined the school in Highbury that Harriet Smith attended. She described Mrs Goddard's school as

a real, honest, old-fashioned boarding-school, where a reasonable quantity of accomplishments were sold at a reasonable price, and where girls might be sent to be out of the way, and scramble themselves into a little education, without any danger of coming back prodigies. Mrs Goddard's school was in high repute and very deservedly, for Highbury was reckoned a particularly healthy spot; she had an ample house and garden, gave the children plenty of wholesome food, let them run about a great deal in the summer, and in winter dressed their chilblains with her own hands.[24]

The school that Jane and her sister attended was the Reading Ladies Boarding School, which was run by a Mrs La Tournelle, whose real name was Sarah Hackitt. This private school for daughters of the clergy and minor gentry was renowned for its 'kindly atmosphere'. The school, housed partly in the ancient gateway of a former Benedictine abbey and partly in a more modern adjoining two-storey building, was surrounded by extensive attractive gardens. The school uniform was a dark dress, a pinafore and a plain cap.

Lessons, which were taught by a Miss Pitts, took place in the mornings only, leaving the girls with plenty of free time. Discipline at the school appears not to have been very strict, as the Austen sisters and their cousin were allowed out occasionally to dine with their brothers at a local inn. It was while at this school that Jane probably began to read the work of contemporary novelists, including Fanny Burney and Maria Edgeworth. The pupils were allowed to borrow books from a local circulating library, and it is likely that this was where Jane found the novels.

Jane left no description of her experience at Mrs La Tournelle's school, but a pupil who attended the school a few years later wrote about her time there. Mary Butt, later the children's author Mrs Sherwood, recalled that 'the greater part of the house was encompassed by a beautiful old-fashioned garden, where the young ladies were allowed to wander under tall trees in hot summer evenings'.[25]

She left the following descriptions of Mrs La Tournelle and her parlour at the school:

a person of the old school – a stout person hardly under seventy, but very active, although she had a cork leg. She had never been seen or known to have changed the fashion of her dress. Her white muslin handkerchief was always pinned with the same number of pins, her muslin apron always hung in the same form; she always wore the same short sleeves, cuffs, and ruffles, with a breast bow to answer the bow in her cap, both being flat with two notched ends.

Mrs La Tournelle received me in a wainscoted parlour, the wainscot a little tarnished, while the room was hung round with chenille pieces representing tombs and weeping willows. A screen in cloth-work stood in a corner, and there were several miniatures over the lofty mantel-piece.[26]

Mrs Sherwood described her stay at the school as 'a very happy one' and 'particularly delightful'.[27] She attributed this to 'the ease and liveliness of the mode of life' there.[28] There is no reason to doubt that Jane also enjoyed her time at the school, not least because of the reassuring presence of her beloved sister. The Austen sisters probably received more attention at school than their hard-pressed mother could have provided at home.

Jane's formal education ended at the age of eleven, when she and Cassandra left the school in Reading and went home to Steventon. They returned to a smaller household as, by that time, there were fewer pupils at the rectory and Frank Austen had left home, at the age of twelve, to enter the Royal Naval Academy in Portsmouth. This was the beginning of a long and illustrious career in the Navy for Jane's 'self-contained and steadfast' brother. The rectory must have been a quieter place without Frank, who was nicknamed Fly by his family because of his boundless energy. James Austen, having gained his B.A. three years earlier, also left Steventon around this time to visit France, and possibly Spain and Holland as well. The only brothers left at home were Henry, who was still being prepared for university, and seven-year-old Charles.

Edward Austen was also on the Continent at this time. His adoptive parents had not sent him to university but on a Grand Tour of Europe to see the classical sights. The Grand Tour was a fashionable way for the sons of the English aristocracy to finish off their education. Edward's tour lasted for two years and included a year in Dresden, where he was received at the Saxon court, and concluded in Rome. He returned with much to tell his family at Steventon.

2

JUVENILIA
1787–1793

Once back in the family home, Jane's real education began. George Austen and his wife were enlightened parents, and wanted their daughters to have a better education than the limited one prescribed for girls at that time. Having reduced the hours he spent teaching private pupils, George Austen now had time to devote himself to educating his intelligent daughters. This scholarly man, with his placid, patient, serene and gentle temperament, was particularly suited to teaching. Jane, who later wrote of her father's 'indescribable tenderness' and 'sweet benevolent smile', was always close to him. Their bond was no doubt strengthened during the years in which her father tutored her. The education Jane received from her father was an excellent preparation for a writer. This preparation was described by her brother Henry, in his *Biographical Notice of the Author*, attached to the two novels published after Jane's death, in the following words: 'Being not only a profound scholar, but possessing an exquisite taste in every species of literature, it is not wonderful that his daughter Jane should, at a very early age, have been sensible to the charms of style, and enthusiastic in the cultivation of her own language.'[1]

Jane was allowed free rein in her father's large, well-stocked library and she made good use of this resource. Her reading included the works of Shakespeare, Samuel Johnson, the racy novels of Smollett, Richardson and Fielding, the poetry of Crabbe and Cowper, and the essays in *The Spectator* and other periodicals. Jane's clever, Oxford-educated brother James helped to direct her reading and form her taste in literature. Henry Austen wrote that it was 'difficult to say at what age she was not intimately acquainted with the merits and defects of the best essays and novels in the English language'.[2] Despite being such an avid reader, Jane later regretted that she had not read more in her youth.

William and Richard Austen-Leigh described the education Jane received at home in *Jane Austen, Her Life and Letters, A Family Record*.

> On the whole, she grew up with a good stock of such accomplishments as might be expected of a girl bred in one of the more intellectual of the clerical houses of that day. She read French easily, and knew a little of Italian; and she was well read in the English literature of the eighteenth century. As a child, she had strong political opinions, especially on the affairs of the sixteenth and seventeenth centuries. She was a vehement defender of Charles I and his grandmother, Mary, and did not disdain to make annotations in this sense (which still exist) on the margin of her *Goldsmith's History*. As she grew up, the party politics of the day seem to have occupied very little of her attention, but she probably shared the feeling of moderate Toryism which prevailed in her family.[3]

Mental training also formed an important part of Jane's education. There is no doubt that her clever family helped her to develop an enquiring mind and the ability to think for herself. Jane's nephew

Edward referred to this in his *Memoir* when he commented that 'she certainly enjoyed that important element of mental training associating at home with persons of cultivated intellect'.[4]

Such mental training was not encouraged in women in the eighteenth century because it was not necessary for the subservient role they were expected to play in a patriarchal society, and may have led to them questioning their lot in life. Jane valued her academic education highly because she knew how disadvantaged women were by the limited conventional female education. Women's education and its influence on their behaviour, decisions, choices and happiness were to be important themes in Jane's novels. The moral and religious instruction, which began in Jane's early childhood, also continued when she returned home from school. Mary Augusta Austen-Leigh described in her biography how Jane was taught to do her 'duty to God and duty to Man', and that her life revolved 'round these twin poles'.[5]

The ornamental accomplishments which the Austen sisters learned at school were not neglected when they returned home. Jane's niece Anna wrote in 1869 that she believed, but could not be certain, that 'a music Master attended at Steventon'.[6] If so he was probably engaged to teach Jane, who, according to another niece, 'had a natural taste' for music, 'played very pretty tunes on the piano'[7] and had a good singing voice. It is thought that Jane played the piano for her own pleasure, rather than to entertain others. The Austen girls probably also received instruction in drawing as Cassandra became a talented artist and, according to her brother Henry, Jane 'had not only an excellent taste for drawing, but, in her earlier days, evinced great power of hand in the management of the pencil'.[8] Mrs Austen contributed to her daughters' instruction by teaching them plain and fancy needlework, and handwriting. Jane considered the latter to be particularly important and was always proud of her own neat handwriting.

A small sitting room was set aside in the rectory for Jane and her sister, to provide them with a private space in which to chat, draw, write, read and sew. Their niece Anna described this room as follows:

> In later times … a sitting room was made upstairs, 'the dressing-room', as they were pleased to call it, perhaps because it opened into a smaller chamber in which my two aunts slept. I remember the common-looking carpet with its chocolate ground, and the painted press with shelves above for books, and Jane's piano, and an oval glass that hung between the windows; but the charm of the room, with its scanty furniture and cheaply-papered walls, must have been, for those old enough to understand it, the flow of native household wit, with all the fun and nonsense of a large and clever family.[9]

In December 1786, a few months after Jane and Cassandra returned home from school, George Austen's now widowed sister Philadelphia paid the family a visit. She was accompanied by her daughter Eliza and infant grandson Hastings, named after Eliza's godfather, Warren Hastings. During this visit Jane became fond of her beautiful, sophisticated and flamboyant cousin Eliza, and developed a close friendship with her which lasted until Eliza's death. Mary Augusta Austen-Leigh provided the following information about Eliza in her biography:

> She was greatly attached to the family at Steventon, especially to her Uncle George, and she with her mother spent much time at the Rectory before she was taken by the latter to finish her education in Paris, where in 1781 she married a French nobleman, Jean Capotte Comte de Feuillide. She was a lovely and accomplished young woman, who went out much into gay and high society both in Paris and London. Her husband's estates

were situated in the south of France, and thither she at one time travelled, making in the course of the summer an expedition across the Pyrenees to take part in the gaieties of the beautiful watering place, Bagneres de Bigorre, on their further side. The affectionate and regular correspondence she maintained with her English relations does not seem to have been diminished by these foreign experiences, and when political thunderclouds gathered over France the Comte dispatched her, with her infant son, to England, to find a safe refuge in Steventon Rectory, where she frequently resided in the dark days that were to follow...[10]

Eliza returned to the rectory the following Christmas and played a leading role in the family theatricals that year.

It was around this time that Jane first began to write. There was already a tradition of writing in her family. Mrs Austen, as well as being an excellent letter writer, also wrote clever epigrammatic verses and even, reputedly, wrote her recipes in verse. James Austen wrote religious and pastoral poetry. During his time at Oxford James edited, and contributed to, *The Loiterer*, a student newspaper written in the style of *The Spectator* and *The Rambler*, the popular periodicals of Addison and Steele. Henry Austen contributed to this publication during his time at the university.

Jane's 'childish effusions', as her nephew Edward described her early writings, or her *Juvenilia*, as they are usually termed, reveal the extent of her reading and understanding of English history and literature, which they often parodied. Jane collected her writing from the years 1787 to 1793 into three copy books which she labelled *Volume the First*, *Volume the Second* and *Volume the Third*. Particularly noteworthy among Jane's early essays, plays, stories and short novels were *Love and Freindship* (sic), completed in 1790 and *Lesley Castle*, written around the year 1792. These two short novels were written in the popular letter form and parodied the contemporary novel of sensibility. Another early work was

The Mystery, An Unfinished Comedy, which was dedicated, with mock solemnity, to George Austen. The humour, wit, comedy and characterisation in these early works anticipated the talent so evident in her novels.

A spoof history book, dated 27 November 1791, shows the breadth of Jane's knowledge of English history. *The History of England From the Reign of Henry the 4th to the Death of Charles 1st By a Partial, Prejudiced and Ignorant Historian* was written with a pro-Stuart bias, and portrayed English history as a tragedy, with Mary, Queen of Scots as a heroine. This book was illustrated by Jane's sister with characters dressed in eighteenth-century costume, and was dedicated to her. The *Juvenilia* was written, as all Jane's works originally were, to be read aloud to her family as a source of amusement and entertainment. In his *Memoir* Edward Austen-Leigh noted that the later pieces of the *Juvenilia* marked a development in Jane's progress as a writer.

> But between these childish effusions, and the composition of her living works, there intervened another stage of her progress, during which she produced some stories, not without merit, but which she never considered worthy of publication. During this preparatory period her mind seems to have been working in a very different direction from that into which it ultimately settled. Instead of presenting faithful copies of nature, these tales were generally burlesques, ridiculing the improbable events and exaggerated sentiments which she had met with in sundry silly romances. Something of this fancy is to be found in *Northanger Abbey*, but she soon left it far behind in her subsequent course. It would seem as if she were first taking note of all the faults to be avoided, and curiously considering how she ought *not* to write before she attempted to put forth her strength in the right direction.[11]

Edward also made the observation that 'however puerile the matter', Jane's *Juvenilia* was 'always composed in pure simple English, quite free from the over-ornamented style which might be expected from so young a writer'.[12]

In some of the longer works belonging to this period, Jane moved away from nonsensical stories mocking contemporary popular novels to more realistic stories of eighteenth-century life. With their domestic settings, themes of courtship, love and marriage, and their clever delineation of character they provided a foretaste of her later mature writing. The unfinished story *Catharine, or The Bower* is a good example of such writing.

It was during this period, when Jane was developing her writing skills, that she first travelled to Kent. In the summer of 1788 George Austen took his wife and daughters to visit his ninety-year-old uncle Francis at Sevenoaks. The Austens also met George's half-brother William and his family. Philadelphia Walter, William's daughter, wrote a letter to her brother describing the meeting. This letter, dated 23 July 1788, contained an unfavourable comparison of the twelve-year-old Jane with her fifteen-year-old sister.

> Yesterday I began an acquaintance with my two female cousins, Austens. My uncle, aunt, Cassandra and Jane arrived at Mr F. Austen's the day before. We dined with them there. As it's pure nature to love ourselves, I may be allowed to give the preference to the eldest, who is generally reckoned a most striking resemblance of me in features, complexion and manners … The youngest Jane is very like her brother Henry, not at all pretty and very prim, unlike a girl of twelve, but it is hasty judgement which you will scold me for. My aunt has lost several fore-teeth, which makes her look old; my uncle is quite white-haired, but looks vastly well; all in high spirits and disposed to be pleased with each other.[13]

Philadelphia added these further comments to the letter a day or so later: 'I continue to admire my amiable likeness the best of the two in every respect; she has kept up conversation in a very sensible and pleasing manner. Yesterday they all spent the day with us, and the more I see of Cassandra the more I admire her, Jane is whimsical and affected.'[14]

The Austens stopped in London on their way home from Kent to visit George's sister Philadelphia Hancock and her daughter Eliza, who were staying in Orchard Street. This was Jane's first recorded visit to London. The unflattering description of Jane by Philadelphia Walter was balanced by the following one, written to her in a letter dated 26 September 1792 by Eliza: 'Cassandra and Jane are both very much grown (the latter is now taller than myself), and greatly improved as well in manners as in person, both of which are now much more formed than when you saw them. They are I think equally sensible and both so to a degree seldom met with, but still my heart gives the preference to Jane, whose kind partiality to me indeed requires a return of the same nature.'[15]

Between 1791 and 1793 a number of events, both happy and distressing, occurred within Jane's immediate and wider family. Firstly, in July 1791, her younger brother Charles left home to enter the Royal Naval Academy in Portsmouth, following in his brother's footsteps. In December of that year Edward Austen married Elizabeth Bridges, daughter of Sir Brook Bridges of Goodnestone Park, near Wingham, Kent. The newly married couple set up home at Rowling, a house near Canterbury belonging to the Bridges family. In February 1792, George Austen's sister Philadelphia died following a prolonged illness. A few weeks later James Austen married Anne Mathew, daughter of General Edward Mathew of Laverstoke Manor House, near Overton. They moved into Deane Rectory and James, who had been an ordained minister for several years, became his father's curate at Deane. Later in 1792 Cassandra Austen became engaged to the Reverend Tom Fowle, a former pupil of her father's. Tom was the son of the Reverend Thomas Fowle, vicar of Kintbury in Berkshire.

The year 1793 began happily, with the birth of Edward and Elizabeth Austen's first child, Fanny, in January. This happiness was soon clouded, however, by news of the dangerous political situation in France following the execution of Louis XVI, leading to fears for the safety of Eliza de Feuillide's husband. In February, the new republican government declared war on Britain and Holland. Two months later Henry Austen became a lieutenant in the Oxfordshire militia, and James and Anne Austen's daughter, Jane Anna Elizabeth, known as Anna, was born. This year was also important because it was the year in which Jane completed the writing that is collectively known as her *Juvenilia*, and began to write the first drafts of two of the novels which were to earn her worldwide fame and recognition.

3

THE PARSON'S DAUGHTER
1794–1796

As well as helping their mother to run the family home, Jane and Cassandra Austen, like other clergy daughters, assisted their father in his ministry to the poor. Unlike many eighteenth-century clergymen, George Austen lived among his parishioners and took his duties towards them seriously. The Austen sisters regularly visited the poor and sick of their father's parish, and made and collected clothes for the needy. Jane later drew on her experience of visiting the poor when she described the chaotic, overcrowded conditions in which the Price family lived in her novel *Mansfield Park*. This experience probably inspired the concern for the poor, and the belief that they should be treated kindly and respectfully, which is expressed in the novel *Emma*.

It was not just her duty as the parson's daughter which prompted Jane to help the poor; she was also motivated by her strong Christian faith. Jane was probably confirmed into the Anglican Church at the age of nineteen, as a prayer book still exists with her name written in it and the date of 24 April 1794. She attended services at her father's church twice every Sunday and took part in daily devotions at home. Jane's strong religious faith and her piety were undoubtedly due to the example set by her parents, as well as by the moral and religious training she had received from early childhood. Edward Austen-Leigh described Jane as 'a humble and believing Christian',[1] and Henry Austen described her as 'thoroughly religious and devout' with opinions which 'accorded strictly with those of our established Church'.[2] The following extract from a prayer written by Jane, which still hangs on the wall of St Nicholas church in Steventon, demonstrates her beliefs and piety: 'Give us almighty father, so to pray, as to deserve to be heard, to address thee with our hearts, as with our lips. Thou art everywhere present, from thee no secret can be hid. May the knowledge of this teach us to fix our thoughts on thee, with reverence and devotion that we pray not in vain.'

Jane continued to fill her free time at home with the occupations she enjoyed most – needlework or 'work' as it was called, reading, playing the piano and writing. Outside the home Jane enjoyed trips to Basingstoke to go shopping, taking long walks in the countryside and visiting friends and neighbours with Cassandra, her constant companion. In wet weather the sisters wore wooden pattens over their shoes to protect them, and to keep their long dresses out of muddy puddles.

In the evenings Jane often attended social functions. She particularly liked events which included dancing, both impromptu dances at small gatherings and larger dances held in private homes, or at the Basingstoke Assembly Rooms. Edward Austen-Leigh described, in some detail, the dances which his aunt enjoyed so much as a young woman.

There must have been more dancing throughout the country in those days than there is now; and it seems to have sprung up more spontaneously, as if it were a natural production, with less fastidiousness as to the quality of music, lights and floor. Many country towns had a monthly ball throughout the winter, in some of which the same apartment served for dancing and tea-room. Dinner parties more frequently ended with an extempore dance on the carpet, to the music of a harpsichord in the house, or a fiddle from the village. This was always supposed to be for the entertainment of the young people, but many, who had little pretension to youth, were very ready to join in it. There can be no doubt that Jane herself enjoyed dancing, for she attributes this taste to her favourite heroines; in most of her works, a ball or a private dance is mentioned, and made of importance.

Many things connected with the ball-rooms of those days have now passed into oblivion ... But the stately minuet still reigned supreme; and every regular ball commenced with it. It was a slow and solemn movement, expressive of grace and dignity, rather than of merriment. It abounded in formal bows and courtesies, with measured paces, forwards, backwards, and sideways, and many complicated gyrations. It was executed by one lady and gentleman, amidst the admiration, or the criticism of surrounding spectators ... Hornpipes, cotillions and reels, were occasionally danced: but the chief occupation of the evening was the interminable country dance, in which all could join. This dance presented a great show of enjoyment.[3]

The county balls, which Jane often attended, were held on Thursday once a month during the season. Constance Hill went in search of the old Basingstoke Assembly Rooms when she was researching her biography, a century after Jane frequented them. She found the building formerly used as the Assembly Rooms behind 'The Angel' inn; at that time it was being used as a hay-loft. In her book Constance Hill described how she imagined the Assembly Rooms must have appeared to Jane and her fellow dancers.

We mount some wooden steps leading up to the so-called hay-loft, and in another moment we find ourselves in the old

Assembly Rooms. Piles of hay cover the floor, but we cannot mistake the place. There are the handsome chimney-pieces, the sash windows and the double flap doors that mark a reception-room of importance; and when we push aside the litter beneath our feet, the fine even planking of a dancing floor appears. As we gaze around us, the discoloured and mouldering plaster on the walls, the broken panes, the cobweb festoons, the forlorn and rusty grates, and the piles of hay all vanish, and we seem to see the room as it appeared in its palmy days when prepared for a county ball. A chandelier, resplendent with wax candles, hangs in the middle of the room. Its lights are reflected in the polished floor beneath and again in the oval mirrors above the two chimney-pieces. Fires are blazing in the hearths. See, there are the musicians, in their tie-wigs and knee-breeches, just entering, and soon the gay company will be arriving.[4]

The people Jane met at social functions provided her with excellent material for the stories she was writing, and for her future novels. She seemed to be able to detach herself from what was going on around her and adopt the viewpoint of an outsider. The fact that Jane was slightly lower in the social scale than most of the people she mixed with probably made her feel as if she did not quite belong, and made it easier for her to step back. Being detached enabled her to make judgements and observations she may otherwise have missed. Jane's dual role, as participator and observer at social events, was invaluable to her as a writer. She became a careful and critical observer of people's foibles, weaknesses, manners and habits, and developed a writer's fascination with the behaviour and motives of the people around her. According to William and Richard Austen-Leigh, Jane inherited her acute powers of observation from her mother and other important qualities from her father; 'If one may divide qualities which often overlap, one would be inclined to surmise that Jane Austen inherited from her father her serenity of mind, the refinement of her intellect, her delicate appreciation of style, while her mother supplied the acute observation of character, and the wit and humour, for which she was equally distinguished.'[5]

Jane spent much time developing her writing skills during this period. The short novel *Lady Susan* was probably begun around 1794. It was written in the popular letter form, with which Jane had been familiar since she first started reading contemporary fiction. This novel is about a cruel mother who tried, but failed, to force her daughter into a marriage she did not want. The idea is believed to have come from the sad tale of the unhappy childhood of Mrs Lloyd, the Austen family friend who lived at Deane Rectory until 1792. The main character is thought to have been based on Mrs Lloyd's mother, who cruelly mistreated her children. *Lady Susan*, which according to her family the author never intended to be published, did not appear in print until 1870, when it was published in the same volume as Edward Austen-Leigh's biography. William and Richard Austen-Leigh wrote the following comments on *Lady Susan* in their biography:

As a stage in the development of the author it has great interest. Strictly speaking, it is not a story but a study. There is hardly any attempt at a plot, or at the grouping of various characters; such as exist are kept in the background, and serve chiefly to bring into bolder relief the one full-length, highly finished, wholly sinister figure which occupies the canvas, but which seems, with the completion of the study, to have disappeared entirely from the mind of its creator. It is equally remarkable that an inexperienced girl should have had independence and boldness enough to draw at full length a woman of the type of Lady Susan, and that, after she had done so, the purity of her imagination and the delicacy of her taste should have prevented her from ever repeating the experiment.[6]

In 1795 Jane began to write *Elinor and Marianne,* an early version of the novel later published as *Sense and Sensibility. Elinor and Marianne* was also written in the epistolary form, but this was changed to a straightforward narrative by the time the novel had evolved into its final form. By October 1796 Jane was working on *First Impressions,* which was eventually to become her most famous novel, *Pride and Prejudice.*

As well as writing fiction, Jane was a prolific letter writer. Letter writing, the only way of keeping in touch with distant family and friends, was an important occupation for women in Georgian England. Many of the female characters in Jane's novels write letters and she sometimes used this as a device to move the plot along. Jane's talent for writing amusing and interesting letters delighted her family and friends. The majority of Jane's letters were written to her sister; Jane and Cassandra wrote to each other several times a week when they were apart. These periods spent apart became increasingly frequent, as the sisters started to stay separately with their brother and sister-in-law in Kent. Jane's first visit to Kent by herself took place in the summer of 1794.

In her *Memoir* Caroline Austen wrote the following paragraph regarding her aunt's letters:

> They were very well expressed, and they must have been very interesting to those who received them – but they detailed chiefly home and family events: and she seldom committed herself *even* to an opinion – so that to strangers they could be *no* transcript of her mind – they would not feel that they knew her any the better for having read them – They were rather *over*cautious, for excellence. Her letters to Aunt Cassandra (for they were sometimes separated) were, I dare say, open and confidential – My Aunt looked over them and burnt the greater part (as she told me), 2 or 3 years before her own death – She left, or gave some as legacies to the Nieces – but of those that *I* have seen, several had portions cut out.[7]

William and Richard Austen-Leigh explained why Cassandra destroyed so many of her sister's letters.

> The Austens had a great hatred and dread of publicity. Cassandra felt this with especial force, and the memory of Jane was to her so sacred that to allow the gaze of strangers to dwell upon the actions or the feelings of so precious a being would have seemed to her nothing short of profanation. In her old age she became aware that Jane's fame had not only survived but increased, and that a time might come when the public would wish to know more details of her life than had been given in the short memoir, written by Henry Austen, and prefixed to her posthumous works. Cassandra would not indeed be likely to think it possible that the letters themselves should be published, but they might be made use of as materials and so she determined to do what must have been a great sacrifice, and burn all those which were specially dear to herself, feeling confident that the remainder would not be disturbed.[8]

The surviving letters from Jane to Cassandra, although just part of one side of their correspondence and telling only what happened when they were apart, are a fascinating source of information about much of Jane's adult life.

Jane's earliest surviving letters to her sister describe her first romantic attachment, an important event in her life. Jane, who already had a reputation for being flirtatious, was aware that girls of her social class were expected to marry and become mothers and home-makers. With very few opportunities for respectable female employment in Georgian England, marriage was the only way for a young woman to become independent of her family and achieve a role and status in life. There was also a stigma attached to being a spinster, and a woman was considered an old maid if she was not married by her mid-twenties. Jane would also have been aware that her marriage prospects were blighted because her father was not wealthy enough to provide her with a marriage portion, making her less attractive to potential suitors. The plots of all Jane's novels revolve around the serious subject of finding a suitable husband.

Jane's first romance was with a young man named Tom Lefroy. In December 1795 Tom travelled to Hampshire, from his home in Ireland, to pay a visit to his uncle the Reverend George Lefroy, whose wife Anne was Jane's close friend. Jane met Tom on a number of social occasions during the weeks he stayed in Ashe, and a mutual affection developed. It seems that the Lefroys noticed the growing attachment with alarm. The reason for their concern was that Tom was an impecunious young man whose education was being paid for by a wealthy relative. Tom was planning a career in law and it was feared that, if he became engaged to a young lady without financial means, he would lose the support of his benefactor. The Lefroys, therefore, acted quickly to bring the budding romance to an end and early in the new year Tom was dispatched back to Ireland.

Two letters sent by Jane to Cassandra, who was away from home at the time, describe her last three meetings with Tom. In a letter dated 9–10 January 1796, Jane described how she danced with Tom at a ball.

You scold me so much in the nice long letter which I have this moment received from you, that I am almost afraid to tell you how my Irish friend and I behaved. Imagine to yourself everything most profligate and shocking in the way of dancing and sitting down together. I *can* expose myself, however, only *once more*, because he leaves the country soon after next Friday, on which day we *are* to have a dance at Ashe after all. He is a very gentleman-like, good-looking, pleasant young man, I assure you. But as to our having ever met, except at the last three balls, I cannot say much; for he is so excessively laughed at about me at Ashe, that he is afraid of coming to Steventon, and ran away when we called on Mrs Lefroy a few days ago.[9]

Jane was aware that she had exposed herself to gossip by dancing and sitting down with Tom so much. If a couple spent too much time together, instead of dancing with a number of different partners, it was soon assumed that they had reached an 'agreement'.

In the second part of this letter Jane added, 'After I had written the above, we received a visit from Mr Tom Lefroy and his cousin George. The latter is really very well-behaved now and, as for the other, he has but *one* fault, which time will, I trust, entirely remove – it is that his morning coat is a great deal too light. He is a very great admirer of Tom Jones and therefore wears the same coloured clothes, I imagine, which *he* did when he was wounded.'[10]

This rather flippant tone, with its reference to the hero of Henry Fielding's novel, could well have been a cover for Jane's true feelings. In her next letter, dated 14 to 15 January 1796, Jane told Cassandra that she would be meeting Tom the following night at a ball at Ashe. She rather intriguingly continued, 'I look forward with great impatience to it, as I rather expect to receive an offer from my friend in the course of the evening. I shall refuse him, however, unless he promises to give away his white coat.'[11]

The light-heartedness of Jane's letter makes it difficult to decide whether she really expected an offer of marriage that night. She went on to say that she intended to 'confine' herself in future to Tom Lefroy, but also added that she did not 'care sixpence' for him. On the day of the ball Jane wrote, 'At length the Day is come on which I am to flirt my last with Tom Lefroy, & when you receive this it will be over – My tears flow as I write, at the melancholy idea.'[12]

There seems to be an underlying sadness in this letter – a suspicion that, despite her description of this attachment as no more than a flirtation and that she did not care for him, Jane really did shed tears when Tom returned to Ireland. It was not long before Tom Lefroy met and married a wealthy heiress, which would seem to confirm that Jane's first romantic attachment was indeed halted because of her lack of a dowry. Tom went on to enjoy a glittering career in the legal profession.

In his *Memoir*, Edward Austen-Leigh wrote the following paragraph about his aunt's romance with Tom.

At Ashe also Jane became acquainted with a member of the Lefroy family, who was still living when I began these memoirs, a few months ago; the Right Hon. Thomas Lefroy, the late Chief Justice of Ireland. One must look back more than seventy years to reach the time when these two bright young persons were, for a short time, intimately acquainted with each other, and then separated on their several courses, never to meet again; both destined to attain some distinction in their different ways, one to survive the other for more than half a century, yet in his extreme old age to remember and speak, as he sometimes did, of his former companion, as one to be much admired, and not easily forgotten by those who had known her.[13]

Tom's nephew was recorded as saying that his uncle admitted to having been 'in love' with Jane, but that 'it was a boyish love'. Caroline Austen supplied her brother Edward with the following information about their aunt's first romance:

That there was *something* in it, is true – but nothing out of the common way – (as *I* believe). Nothing to call ill usage, and no very serious sorrow endured … I have *my* story from my Mother, who was near at the time … If *his* love had continued a few more years, he *might* have sought her out again – as he was *then* making enough to marry on – but who can wonder that he did *not*? He was settled in Ireland, and he married an Irish lady – who certainly *had* the convenience of *money* – there was *no* engagement, and never *had* been.[14]

Nevertheless, Jane did not forget Tom quickly. Several references to him in later letters show that she was interested in hearing about him for some time after they parted, but there is no record of her reaction to his marriage.

Jane's early letters to Cassandra also described a visit to the home of her brother Edward and his wife. She was accompanied on the long journey from Hampshire to Kent by Edward and their brother Frank. Jane was always accompanied on journeys by a male relative, as it was considered neither safe nor seemly for a young lady to travel alone in Georgian England. Jane's letters from Kent described her socialising with the local gentry and aristocracy, as well as enjoying the company of Elizabeth Austen's family, the Bridges of Goodnestone Park. On 5 September, Jane wrote, 'We dined at Goodnestone & in the Evening danced two Country Dances and the Boulangeries. – I opened the Ball with Edwd Bridges; the other couples, were Lewis Cage & Harriot, Frank and Louisa, Fanny & George. Elizabth played one Country dance, Lady Bridges the other, which she made Henry dance with her; and Miss Finch played the Boulangeries … We supped there, & walked home at night under the shade of two Umbrellas.'[15]

Visits to Kent were a pleasure to Jane because her 'kind-hearted and affectionate' brother was such good company. Edward, who had a lively, fun-loving side to his personality, was also an excellent host who always ensured that his guests had a good time. Jane also enjoyed the pleasure of the company of Edward's young family.

A number of significant family events occurred during this period of Jane's life. In February 1794 the Comte de Feuillide, the husband of Jane's cousin Eliza, lost his life during the Reign of Terror in France. This tragic loss affected the young Jane. According to William and Richard Austen-Leigh 'it was an event to make a lasting impression on a quick-witted and emotional girl of eighteen, and Eliza remained so closely linked to the family that the tragedy probably haunted Jane's memory for a long time to come'.[16]

Having lost both her mother and her husband, Eliza found herself alone with an invalid son to care and provide for. As a result she became more dependent on her Hampshire relatives and spent more time with them at Steventon.

In May of the following year Anne Austen, the wife of Jane's brother James, died. Her grieving husband sent his young daughter, Anna, to be comforted and cared for by her grandparents and aunts at Steventon Rectory. Jane's closeness to Anna dated back to this time when she helped to look after her motherless niece. Anna spent most of the next two years at her grandparents' home. A little cherry-wood chair was bought for her to use.

Jane's favourite brother Henry was awarded his Master of Arts degree in January 1796, around the time that his sister Cassandra's fiancé, Tom Fowle, set sail for the West Indies. Tom went as the private chaplain of his kinsman Lord Craven who, as colonel of the Regiment of Foot, left England to join Lord Abercromby's regiment. As the rector of a small parish in Wiltshire, Tom did not earn enough money to support a wife. He planned to save sufficient money on his trip to the West Indies to enable him to marry Cassandra on his return.

The careers of Jane's sailor brothers flourished during these years. In September 1796 Frank was appointed commander of the *Triton*, a new frigate recently launched at Deptford, and Charles, having been involved for some time in the war with France, became lieutenant on board the *Scorpion*.

4

THE EARLY WRITING PERIOD
1797–1800

In January 1797, the widowed James Austen married Mary Lloyd. This marriage was welcomed by the Austen family, as recorded by Eliza de Feuillide, who was herself the object of James's affections for a brief period. 'James has chosen a second wife in the person of Miss Mary Lloyd, who is not either rich or handsome, but very sensible and good humoured. Jane seems much pleased with the match, and it is natural she should, having long known and liked the lady.'[1]

The couple moved into Deane parsonage, where Mary had previously lived with her mother and sister, and little Anna Austen joined them there. The family at Steventon Rectory must have missed the presence of the lively child, especially her aunt Jane, with whom she had developed a close bond.

A few weeks later the Austens were overcome with grief at the news that Cassandra's fiancé Tom Fowle had died of yellow fever at San Domingo, just before he was due to return home. In a letter to her cousin dated 3 May 1797, Eliza de Feuillide described the tragedy as 'a very severe stroke to the whole family, and particularly to poor Cassandra, for whom I feel more than I can express. Indeed I am most severely grieved at this event, and the pain which it must occasion our worthy relations. Jane says that her sister behaves with a degree of resolution and propriety which no common mind could evince in so trying a situation.'[2] Edward Austen-Leigh described this as 'a great and lasting grief' to his aunt, who was comforted at this time by Jane and strengthened by her deep religious faith. Tom left Cassandra enough money to give her a measure of financial security, but she remained unmarried for the rest of her life.

The year 1797 was an important one in Jane's writing career, as in August she finished the manuscript of *First Impressions*, after ten months of writing. Jane's niece Anna was present when this novel was read aloud to the family, as recorded in a letter written to her half-brother when he was compiling information for his biography. 'I have been told that one of her earliest Novels (*Pride and Prejudice*) was read aloud (in M.S. of course) in the Parsonage at Deane, whilst I was in the room, & not expected to listen – Listen however I did, with so much interest, & with so much talk afterwards about "Jane and Elizabeth" that it was resolved, for prudence sake, to read no more of the story aloud in my hearing.'[3]

Jane was anxious from the outset to keep her novel writing a secret from all but her closest family, possibly because novels were looked down on as a form of literature and perhaps also from modesty.

The Reverend Austen was so impressed with Jane's work that he sent the manuscript to the London publisher Thomas Cadell in November 1797, with the following letter:

Sir, – I have in my possession a manuscript novel, comprising 3 vols; about the length of Miss Burney's *Evelina*. As I am well aware of what consequence it is that a work of this sort shd make its first appearance under a respectable name, I apply to you. I shall be much obliged therefore if you will inform me whether you choose to be concerned in it, what will be the expense of publishing it at the author's risk; and what you will venture to advance for the property of it, if on perusal it is approved of? Should you give any encouragement, I will send you the work.

I am, Sir, your humble servant,

George Austen[4]

Cadell declined the invitation to read the manuscript by return of post. He thus, unwittingly, rejected the novel later published as *Pride and Prejudice*, which brought its author worldwide acclaim and such a prominent place in English literature. In her letter to Edward, Anna made the following comment on George Austen's attempt to get the novel published: 'The letter does not do much credit to the tact or courtesy of our good Grandfather for Cadell was a great man in his day, and it is not surprising that he should have refused the favor (*sic*) so offered from an unknown…'[5]

It is not known whether Jane was aware of her father's action. However, it is unlikely that she would have been upset by this eminent publisher's refusal to read her novel as, at this stage, she was not seeking publication. If Jane was aware of this rejection of her manuscript, it did not stop her from embarking on the rewriting of *Elinor and Marianne* as the narrative novel which was later published under the title of *Sense and Sensibility*.

George Austen always encouraged and supported Jane in her writing. It may have been around this time that he bought her a writing desk in Basingstoke, which was described in the sale particulars as 'a small mahogany writing desk with 1 long Drawer and Glass Ink Stand Compleat'. The desk, which cost twelve shillings, is probably the one belonging to Jane which has been passed down through generations of the Austen family. George Austen may well have encouraged his daughter to develop her writing talent because he knew that her marriage prospects were limited by his inability to provide her with a dowry. He may have thought that writing was Jane's best chance of acquiring an independent income. Writing was considered an acceptable female occupation in Georgian England, and a number of women made money by writing the books which filled the popular circulating libraries.

In November of this year Jane visited Bath with her sister and mother. Mrs Austen was not well at this time, which may have been the reason for their visit to this famous health resort. Bath was still a fashionable destination in the last years of the eighteenth century, although it was gradually being replaced in popularity by Brighton. The attractions of Bath included the assembly rooms, concert halls, pleasure gardens, fashionable shops, and excellent walking locations in the surrounding hills.

The Austen ladies travelled from Steventon via Andover and Devizes. It was raining during the final part of their journey, and their first view of Bath was a wet and gloomy one. They probably stayed with Mrs Austen's brother James Leigh-Perrot and his wife at 1 Paragon, and met many of their wide circle of friends and acquaintances. This visit, which stretched into December, gave Jane ample opportunity to observe the behaviour and manners of the people she met, and provided her with material for her novels.

When Mrs Austen and her daughters arrived home from Bath they were informed that Henry had become engaged to his cousin Eliza, in whom he had shown a romantic interest for some time. At first Eliza had been unwilling to give up her freedom by marrying again, but she had eventually agreed to marry Henry. William and Richard Austen-Leigh described this event in the following paragraph:

On returning home for Christmas, they received a piece of news which, even if it did not come entirely as a surprise, can hardly have given unmixed pleasure. This was the engagement of Henry Austen to his cousin, Eliza de Feuillide, his senior by some ten years. Intended originally for the Church, Henry Austen had abandoned the idea of taking Orders, and had joined the Oxfordshire Militia as lieutenant, in 1793, becoming adjutant and captain four years later. Though he was endowed with many attractive gifts there was a certain infirmity of purpose in his character that was hardly likely to be remedied by a marriage to his very pleasure-loving cousin.[6]

The marriage took place on 31 December.

Shortly before this event Jane's brother Edward came into his inheritance, when his adoptive mother handed over the extensive Knight family estates and properties to him, and retired to Canterbury. Edward and his family moved to Godmersham to live in the grand Palladian-style house, with its beautiful classical interior, which was built in 1732 by Thomas Knight's father. The following description of Godmersham House and estates, taken from Hasted's *History of Kent* (1798), provides an idea of the vast lands and property that Edward inherited in Kent.

It lies in the beautiful Stour valley, a situation healthy and pleasant to the extreme, the River Stour glides through it from Ashford, in its course towards Canterbury; Godmersham house and park are the principal objects in it, both elegant and beautiful, the Ashford high road encircles the east side of the park, along which there is a sunk sence (*sic*), which affords an uninterrupted view of the whole of it, and adds greatly to the beauty of this elegant scene, and leads through the village of Godmersham close to it, the whole village which contains about twenty houses, belongs to Mrs Knight, excepting one house, as does the greatest part of the parish, excepting the lands belonging to the dean and chapter of Canterbury. There are about twenty more houses in the parish, and about two hundred and forty inhabitants in all. The church, and vicarage, a neat dwelling, pleasantly situated, stand at a small distance from the village, on the left side of the road, with the antient (*sic*) manor-house near the former, close to the bank of the river; the meadows in the vale are exceeding fertile, the uplands are chalk, with some gravel among them, the hills rise high on each side, those on the west being the sheep walks belonging to Godmersham-house, the summits of which are finely cloathed (*sic*) with wood, at proper intervals; the opposite ones are the high range of unenclosed pasture downs of Wye and Brabourne.

In addition to this Edward inherited Chawton House and its estate in Hampshire, which included the village of Steventon. Jane was to pay many happy visits to Edward and his family in their new home.

Just before Christmas 1797, Jane's friend Mrs Lefroy introduced her to a young man whom she considered would make her a good husband. The young man concerned was the Reverend Samuel Blackall, a fellow of Emmanuel College, Cambridge, who was staying with the Lefroys at Ashe rectory for Christmas. Mrs Lefroy may well have been trying to make up for putting an end to Jane's romance of the previous year. Her matchmaking attempt was unsuccessful, however, because Jane did not take to Samuel Blackall at all. She was shocked and put off by his pompous manner and self-centred personality. Jane was relieved when the man she described as 'this piece of Perfection, noisy Perfection'[7] left Hampshire soon after.

During the first half of 1798 Jane, according to William and Richard Austen-Leigh, 'was able to devote some happy months of unbroken leisure to writing the first draft of the book known as *Northanger Abbey*'.[8] At this stage *Northanger Abbey*, which is set in Bath, was named *Susan*. Jane's 'happy months' were spoiled, however, by the news of the death of her cousin Jane Williams (*née* Cooper), in August. This was the cousin with whom Jane had gone to boarding school, and whose letter to Mrs Austen relaying news of her illness saved Jane's life. Jane Williams was killed in a carriage accident in Newport on the Isle of Wight. Her death was a great shock to the Austen family, and especially to Jane and Cassandra, who had been close to their cousin since childhood.

Later the same month the Reverend and Mrs Austen, Cassandra and Jane paid their first visit to Edward and his family at their new home in Godmersham. It was Jane's first experience of staying in a grand Georgian country house, and she began to gather material on how a large country house and estate were run, which she would later put to good use in her novel *Mansfield Park*.

Jane was introduced to members of the East Kent aristocracy, who were part of Edward and Elizabeth's new social circle, at a ball she attended at Ashford Assembly Rooms. Mary Augusta Austen-Leigh observed in her biography that Jane's visits to Kent 'must have afforded ample time as well as opportunity to mix in the society of that neighbourhood, where she could observe English country life from a fresh point of view, and could compare it with the corresponding class of society she already knew well in Hampshire, around Steventon'.[9]

Jane always enjoyed the luxurious surroundings, fine food and social events at Godmersham. She once observed that 'Kent is the only place for happiness, everybody is rich there' compared to Hampshire 'where everybody is so horribly poor and economical'.

Jane made herself useful on this long visit by sewing shirts for Edward and entertaining her young nephews and nieces. She was particularly fond of her nephew George, who called himself 'itty Dordy'. A fifth baby, William, was born to Edward and Elizabeth while the Austens were staying with them. When

Jane and her parents left Godmersham in October, Cassandra remained behind to nurse Elizabeth while she recovered from her confinement, and to help run the household. On the journey home, when Jane and her parents stopped for the night at the Bull and George Inn at Dartford, Jane nearly lost her precious writing desk and all its contents. She described what happened in a letter to her sister.

> After we had been here a quarter of an hour it was discovered that my writing and dressing boxes had been by accident put into a chaise which was just packing off as we came in, and were driven away towards Gravesend on their way to the West Indies. No part of my property could have been such a prize before, for in my writing-box was all my worldly wealth, 7 pounds ... Mr Nottley immediately despatched a man and horse after the chaise, and in half an hour's time I had the pleasure of being as rich as ever; they were got about two or three miles off.[10]

Jane wrote to Cassandra again when she arrived home from this visit. Like all of Jane's letters, this one was written in a chatty style, revealing her positive, cheerful personality as well as her wit and humour. It contains the following, which includes an apparently unkind remark about a Hampshire neighbour. 'Mrs Hall of Sherbourn was brought to bed yesterday of a dead child, some weeks before she expected, oweing (*sic*) to a fright. – I suppose she happened unawares to look at her husband.'[11]

This was one of many seemingly cruel comments written by Jane in letters to her sister, which rather contradict the depiction of her in family memoirs as a kind and gentle person. The Austen family insisted that Jane's nasty comments were never meant to hurt anyone. They stated that Jane's letters were written to amuse and inform Cassandra, and were not intended to be read by anyone else. William and Richard Austen-Leigh described

Jane as 'one of the most considerate and least censorious of mortals'[12] and made the following observation: 'Jane, too, was a mistress of subtle irony; the inveterate playfulness which is constantly cropping up in her books appears also in her letters. Secure of her correspondent, she could pass criticisms, impute motives, and imagine circumstances which would have been very far from her nature had she thought it possible that any less perfectly informed third person could see them.'[13]

The Austen-Leighs also observed that 'the correspondence was between sisters who knew, each of them, what the other was thinking, and could feel sure that nothing one might say would be misapprehended by the other; and the sort of freemasonry which results from such a situation adds to the difficulty of perfect comprehension by outsiders'.[14]

Jane's next letter to her sister, dated 17 November 1798, contained the important news of the birth of James-Edward, the first child of James and Mary Austen. This baby was to play an important part in Jane's life, not least as the author of the first biography of her. A few weeks later Jane excitedly relayed another piece of news, which brought the family great pleasure. 'My Dear Cassandra, Frank is made. He was yesterday raised to the Rank of Commander, & appointed to the *Petterel* Sloop, now at Gibraltar. – A Letter from Daysh has just announced this, & as it is confirmed by a very friendly one from Mr Mathew to the same effect transcribing one from Admiral Gambier to the General, We have no reason to suspect the truth of it.'[15]

In December 1798 there was a sequel to Mrs Lefroy's attempt of the previous year to find a husband for Jane. The Reverend Samuel Blackall was invited to pay another visit to Ashe Rectory, when he would have been likely to encounter Jane and her family again. He had clearly considered that Jane would make him a suitable wife because in his letter replying to the invitation he stated, 'It would give me particular pleasure to have an opportunity of improving my acquaintance with that family (the Austens) – with a hope of creating to myself a nearer interest. But at present I cannot indulge any expectation of it.'[16]

Jane was relieved to hear this, as revealed by the following paragraph in a letter to Cassandra:

> This is rational enough; there is less love and more sense in it than sometimes appeared before, and I am very well satisfied. It will all go on exceedingly well, and decline away in a very reasonable manner. There seems no likelihood of his coming into Hampshire this Christmas, and it is therefore most probable that our indifference will soon be mutual, unless his regard, which appeared to spring from knowing nothing of me at first, is best supported by never seeing me. Mrs Lefroy made no remarks on the letter, nor did she indeed say anything about him as relative to me. Perhaps she thinks she has said too much already.[17]

This episode seems to have been no more than a source of amusement to Jane, although she was interested to hear, some years later, that Samuel Blackall had found himself a wife.

Jane met many other men at social events over this busy Christmas period. She had no problems attracting admirers and was never short of dancing partners. This was no doubt due to her physical attractiveness, neat appearance and lively personality. Caroline Austen noted in her memoir that, as a young woman, her aunt 'was not, I beleive (*sic*), an absolute beauty, but before she left Steventon she was established as a very pretty girl, in the opinion of most of her neighbours…'[18]

One ball which Jane attended at Basingstoke Assembly Rooms in December 1798, with her friend Catherine Bigg, was described in detail to Cassandra. 'There were twenty Dances & I danced them all, & without any fatigue – I was glad to find myself capable of dancing so much & with so much satisfaction as I did; – from my slender enjoyment of the Ashford Balls, (as Assemblies for dancing) I had not thought myself equal to it, but in cold weather & with few couples I fancy I could just as well dance for a week together as for half an hour. – My black Cap was openly admired by Mrs Lefroy, & secretly I imagine by every body else in the room.'[19]

After this ball Jane went to stay, as she often did following a Basingstoke ball, at Manydown Park, Catherine's home between Steventon and Basingstoke. Jane's busy social life continued into the new year. On 8 January 1799 she attended a ball at Kempshott House given by Lady Dorchester. She wrote to her sister at Godmersham on the day of the ball, 'I am not to wear my white sattin (*sic*) cap tonight after all; I am to wear a Mamalouc cap instead, which Charles Fowle sent to Mary, & which she lends me. – It is all the fashion now, worn at the Opera, & by Lady Mildmays at Hackwood Balls…'[20]

The craze for Egyptian-style clothes, such as the cap referred to in the letter, was started in England following the Battle of the Nile in August 1798. Jane sent Cassandra the following amusing account of the Kempshott ball:

I do not think I was very much in request – People were rather apt not to ask me till they could not help it; – One's consequence you know varies so much at times without any particular reason. There was one Gentleman, an officer of the Cheshire, a very good-looking young Man, who I was told wanted very much to be introduced to me;– but as he did not want it quite enough to take much trouble in effecting it, We never could bring it about. –I danced with Mr John Wood again, twice with a Mr South a lad from Winchester who I suppose is as far from being related to the Bishop of that Diocese as it is possible to be, with G. Lefroy, & J. Harwood, who I think takes to me rather more than he used to do. – One of my gayest actions was sitting down two Dances in preference to having Lord Bolton's eldest son for my Partner, who danced too ill to be endured.[21]

Constance Hill visited the scene of this ball at Kempshott House near Dummer, and wrote the following description of it: 'We found it to be a stone classical structure such as Miss Austen describes as "a modern residence". It has a large bowed centre, three windows wide, supported by a colonnade of pillars ... The present drawing room, it seems, forms a part of the former ball-room. The house stands on the slope of a hill, and is so built that there is one storey less at the back than the front. In former times the main entrance was at the back, and there the carriages must have set down the gay company for the ball.'[22]

On 16 May 1799 Edward Austen, who was suffering from gout, set off for Bath to take the waters accompanied by his wife, two of his children, his mother and Jane. The journey to Bath, and the party's accommodation in Queen Square, was described in a long letter from Jane to her sister in Steventon.

Our Journey yesterday went off exceedingly well; nothing occurred to alarm or delay us; – We found the roads in excellent order, had very good horses all the way, & reached Devizes with ease by 4 o'clock ... Well, here we are at Bath; we got here about one o'clock, & have been arrived just long enough to go over the house, fix on our rooms, & be very well pleased with the whole of it. ... We are exceedingly pleased with the House; the rooms are quite as large as we expected, Mrs Bromley (the landlady) is a fat woman in mourning, & a little black kitten runs about the Staircase ... we have two very nice sized rooms, with dirty Quilts & everything comfortable. I have the outward & larger apartment, as I ought to have; which is quite as large as our bed room at home, & my Mother's is not materially less. – The Beds are both as large as any at Steventon; & I have a very nice chest of Drawers & a Closet full of shelves – so full indeed that there is nothing else in it, & should therefore be called a Cupboard rather than a Closet I suppose.[23]

The arrival of Edward and Elizabeth Austen of Godmersham Park in Kent and their relatives would have been announced in the list of arrivals published in the Bath newspaper, and recorded in the visitors' books at the various venues the party visited. While Edward took the waters for the benefit of his health, the Austen ladies enjoyed all the pleasures and entertainments which Bath had to offer, including Sydney Gardens, the theatre and the assembly rooms. The Austens also joined Jane's uncle and aunt at various functions and gatherings. Jane was, therefore, provided with plenty of opportunities to collect more material for her writing, by watching and listening to the people around her. The following excerpts from letters written by Jane to Cassandra provide some interesting details of her visit, and a fascinating snapshot of Bath at the end of the eighteenth century.

Sunday 2nd June 1799

What must I tell you of Edward? –Truth or Falsehood ?– I will try the former, & you may chuse (*sic*) for yourself another time. – He was better yesterday than he had been for two or three days before, about as well as while he was at Steventon. – He drinks at the Hetling Pump, is to bathe tomorrow, & try Electricity on Tuesday; – he proposed the latter himself to Dr Fellowes, who made no objection to it, but I fancy we are all unanimous in expecting no advantage from it.

I saw some Gauzes at a shop in Bath Street yesterday at only 4*s* a yard, but they were not so good or so pretty as mine. – Flowers are very much worn, & fruit is still more the thing. – Eliz: has a bunch of Strawberries, & I have seen Grapes, Cherries, Plumbs & Apricots.[24]

I spent Friday evening with the Mapletons, & was obliged to submit to being pleased inspite of my inclination. We took a very charming walk from 6 to 8 up Beacon Hill, & across some fields to the Village of Charlcombe, which is sweetly situated in a little green Valley, as a Village with such a name ought to be ... There is to be a grand gala on Tuesday evening in Sydney Gardens;– a Concert, with Illuminations & fireworks; – to the latter Eliz: & I look forward with pleasure, & even the Concert will have more than its' usual charm with me, as the Gardens are large enough for me to get pretty well beyond the reach of its sound…[25]

Tuesday 11th June 1799

We walked to Weston one evening last week, & liked it very much. – Liked *what* very much? Weston? – no – *walking* to Weston – I have not expressed myself properly, but I hope you will understand me. – We have not been to any public place lately, nor performed anything out of the common daily routine of No. 13 Queen Sq. Bath–. But to day we were to have dashed away at a very extraordinary rate, by dining out, had it not so happened that we do not go.[26]

Wednesday 19th June 1799

Last Sunday We all drank tea in Paragon; my Uncle is still in his flannels, but is getting better again. – On Monday, Mr Evelyn was well enough for us to fulfil our engagement with him; – the visit was very quiet & uneventful; pleasant enough. – We met only another Mr Evelyn, his cousin, whose wife came to Tea. – Last night we were in Sidney Gardens again, as there was a repetition of the Gala which went off so ill on the 4th. – We did not go till nine, & then were in very good time for the Fire-works, which were really beautiful, & surpassing my expectation; – the illuminations too were very pretty. – The weather was as favourable, as it was otherwise a fortnight ago. – The Play on Saturday is I *hope* to conclude our Gaieties here, for nothing but a lengthened stay will make it otherwise.[27]

The Austens left Bath on the 26 June after an enjoyable visit, and with Edward's health restored.

Jane would have had no time to spend on novel writing during her stay in Bath, but she is believed to have finished *Susan* when she returned home. The manuscript was then put away to be revised later; it remained untouched for nearly four years. *First Impressions,* meanwhile, was being read with much pleasure by family and friends.

This busy year continued for the Austens with three late summer visits to relatives in different parts of the country. They visited the Leighs at Adlestrop in Warwickshire, the Coopers at Harpsden in Oxfordshire, and the Cookes at Great Bookham in Surrey. Jane may well have taken her portable writing desk to keep herself occupied during the long hours she spent on the road. The extensive travelling undertaken by Jane in 1799, and the varied scenes she encountered, disprove the claims of some early biographers that she led a sheltered life, largely confined to the quiet backwaters of rural Hampshire.

Another myth about Jane Austen, which was started by some early biographers, including her nephew, was that she led a calm and untroubled life. Jane's life, like that of most people, was touched by trouble and tragedy. In addition to the anxieties and losses previously described, an event occurred in December 1799 which caused great grief to the Austen family. Mrs Austen's sister-in-law, Jane Leigh-Perrot, was accused of stealing a piece of lace from a shop in Bath. This was an attempt by a bankrupt shopkeeper to extort hush money from her wealthy husband. James Leigh-Perrot, however, refused to pay up and his wife was committed to Ilchester Gaol, with no bail granted, to await trial the following March. Instead of staying in the gaol itself Mrs Leigh-Perrot was kept under house arrest in the gaol-keeper's house, and her husband was allowed to stay with her. The Leigh-Perrots had to suffer the discomfort and indignity of living in an over-crowded, noisy and squalid house. The Austens were very worried because, if found guilty, Mrs Leigh-Perrot faced deportation. William and Richard Austen-Leigh described the effect that this 'monstrous' charge had on Jane's family.

The amazement and indignation of the Steventon party may be imagined. They were too sensible to believe that so mean and objectless a crime should really have been committed by a respectable woman, a near relation of their own, whom they knew intimately; but it was not easy to determine how to show sympathy. Mr. and Mrs. Austen seem at last to have come (no doubt with their daughters' good-will) to the momentous decision mentioned in the following letter, which was addressed to Mrs Leigh-Perrot on January 11th 1800, by her cousin Montague Cholmeley.

'You tell me that your good sister Austen has offered you one or both of her daughters to continue with you during your stay in that vile place, but you decline the kind offer, as you cannot procure them accommodation in the house with you, and you cannot let those elegant young women be your inmates in a prison, nor be subjected to the inconveniences which you are obliged to put up with.'[28]

It must have been a great relief to Jane to be spared a spell in a gaol-keeper's house, but the suffering of her kind and affectionate uncle and his wife grieved her. The Austens were greatly relieved when Mrs Leigh-Perrot was eventually acquitted, after just fifteen minutes of deliberation by a jury.

The letters written by Jane to her sister in 1798 and 1799 reveal that, like most young women, she was interested in clothes and the latest fashions. They contain detailed descriptions of the dresses and accessories worn by the women she met and observed on the streets. The letters also reveal that Jane and Cassandra, unlike their sisters-in-law and friends, could not afford expensive new clothes. The sisters struggled to manage on the limited allowance which their father gave them and had to watch every penny. They often could not afford the most basic items of dress, such as stockings, and had to make do with unfashionable clothes freshened up with new ribbons. Although this must have been embarrassing for Jane, she is very matter-of-fact about it in her letters, and displays no trace of self pity. Despite her own financial circumstances, Jane did all she could to help the poor, as indicated in this excerpt from a letter dated 24 to 26 December 1798: 'Of my charities to the poor since I came home, you shall have a faithful account. – I have given a pr of Worsted Stockgs to Mary Hutchins, Dame Kew, Mary Steevens & Dame Staples; a shift to Hannah Staples, & a shawl to Betty Dawkins; amounting in all to about half a guinea. – But I have no reason to suppose that the Battys *would* accept of anything, because I have not made them the offer.'[29]

Jane's positive and happy personality is evident in her letters. These were characteristics which she shared with her father and her favourite brother Henry, who summed up her character as 'faultless … as nearly as human nature can be', and her temper as 'polished as her wit'.[30] If this makes Jane seem too impossibly good to be true, this description of her is supported by her nephew. In his *Memoir*, Edward Austen-Leigh compared the characters of his aunts. 'They were not exactly alike. Cassandra's was the colder and calmer disposition; she was always prudent and well judging, but with less outward demonstration of feeling and less sunniness of temper than Jane possessed. It was remarked in her family that "Cassandra had the *merit* of having her temper always under command, but that Jane had the *happiness* of a temper that never required to be commanded".'[31]

This period, which was a busy, mainly happy and creatively productive one for Jane, ended with a visit to her friend Martha Lloyd at Ibthorpe. In a letter to Cassandra dated 30 November to 1 December 1800, Jane wrote, 'I have the pleasure of thinking myself a very welcome Guest, & the pleasure of spending my time very pleasantly.'[32]

While Jane was enjoying herself with her friend, however, a decision was made by her parents which resulted in an unwelcome change in her life.

5

BATH
1801–1802

In December 1800 George Austen decided to retire from his position as Rector of Steventon and Deane and move to Bath. His living was to be passed on to his son James, and a new curate installed at Deane. William and Richard Austen-Leigh described how Jane was informed of the impending move as follows: 'Tradition says that when Jane returned home accompanied by Martha Lloyd, the news was abruptly announced by her mother, who thus greeted them: "Well, girls, it is all settled; we have decided to leave Steventon in such a week, and go to Bath"; and that the shock of the intelligence was so great to Jane that she fainted away.'[1]

Caroline Austen recorded that her mother Mary was present when Jane received the news and that she 'was greatly distressed'. Jane's sorrow was caused not only by the prospect of leaving her beloved childhood home and her earliest friends, but also by having to leave the Hampshire countryside described by her nephew as 'the cradle of her genius'. Jane was a country girl and the idea of town life did not appeal to her at all. Cassandra Austen was also sorry to be leaving Steventon. The sisters were not consulted about the move and, being financially dependent on their father, they had no choice but to go wherever their parents took them.

There were several probable reasons why Bath was chosen as the location for their new home. Firstly, the Austens knew Bath well and had close relatives who lived there for much of the year. Bath may also have been chosen on account of the health of both of Jane's elderly parents. Another consideration may have been that Bath was renowned as a good hunting ground for husbands. George Austen and his wife may have seen a move there as a last chance for their daughters to find suitable men to marry. In Georgian England women who were still unmarried by their mid- to late twenties were in danger of being regarded as 'old maids', and stigmatised for not fulfilling their destined role in life.

Jane, with her positive outlook on life, soon decided to make the best of things and busied herself in preparations for the move. In a letter dated 3 to 5 January 1801 to Cassandra, who was staying at Godmersham, Jane wrote cheerfully, 'I get more & more reconciled to the idea of our removal … there is something interesting in the bustle of going away, & the prospect of spending future summers by the Sea or in Wales is very delightful.'[2]

In another letter Jane discussed the various locations in Bath which were being considered for their new home. 'It would be very pleasant to be near Sidney Gardens,' she wrote, 'we might go in the labyrinth every day.'[3]

Nearly all the family's furniture and effects were sold in the weeks before they moved, including Jane's precious piano and 500 volumes of her father's books. There were many farewells to be said to friends, neighbours and parishioners. Jane and her mother left Steventon on 4 May 1801, leaving George Austen and Cassandra to join them a few weeks later. Jane's father stayed behind to complete some outstanding business, and her sister paid another visit to Godmersham. Constance Hill in *Jane Austen, Her Homes and Her*

Above left: 1. Sewing was an important female accomplishment in the Georgian period and was one of Jane's favourite pastimes.
Above right: 2. An eighteenth-century pheasant shoot. Jane's brothers enjoyed country sports, including shooting.

3. An eighteenth-century cottage and its occupants. Jane visited the poor who lived in similar cottages in Steventon.

Above: 4. West Front of Abbey Church, Bath , 1788. It is believed that Jane attended services here.
Below: 5. *The Turnpike Gate*. Jane passed through many turnpike gates on her journeys to visit family and friends.
Right: 6. The Roman Baths, Bath. Jane's brother Edward used these baths when he visited the city for his health in 1799.

Above: 7. Queen's Square, Bath, 1784. Jane stayed at 13 Queen's Square when she visited Bath in 1799.
Below: 8. *Dr Oliver and Mr Pierce examining patients in Bath.* Jane's brother Edward consulted the city's physicians in 1799.
Right: 9. Mineral Water Fountain, Bath. This fountain was close to Trim Street where Jane's final home in the city was located.

Above: 10. Royal Crescent, Bath, 1788. This famous crescent, built by John Wood the Younger between 1767 and 1775, was a short walk from all Jane's homes in Bath.
Left: 11. 13 Queen's Square, Bath.
Below left: 12. 1 Paragon, Bath, the home of Jane's uncle James Leigh-Perrot and his wife Jane.

Above: 13. Pulteney Bridge, Bath. Jane crossed this elegant bridge regularly in her walks around Bath. *Right*: 14. 25 Gay Street, Bath, where Jane lived for a few months in 1805. *Below right*: 15. Upper Assembly Rooms, Bath which Jane frequently visited while staying and living in the city.

Above: 16. Royal Crescent, Bath, almost unchanged since Jane lived in the city.
Left: 17. Pump Room, Bath. Jane often accompanied her uncle James Leigh Perrot when he took the waters here.
Below left: 18. Roman Baths, Bath, unchanged since Jane's brother Edward bathed here.

Above: 19. *Baths on the beach at Dawlish.*
Jane visited Dawlish in Devon on a
family holiday in 1802. The Austens
enjoyed several holidays in Devon while
living in Bath.
Right: 20. *A Devonshire Scene, 1798.*
Below: 21. The Holbourne Museum,
Sydney Gardens, Bath. Originally the
Sydney Hotel, this building is close to
Sydney Place where Jane lived from
1801-1804.
Below right: 22. The Jane Austen Centre,
Gay Street, Bath. (Courtesy of the Jane
Austen Centre)

29 & 30. Victorian illustrations of scenes from *Emma*.

Pinned up each other's train for the dance.

The same kind of delicate flattery.

31 & 32. Victorian illustrations of scenes from *Northanger Abbey*.

Looking on her with a face as pallid as her own.

Placed it before Anne.

33 & 34. Victorian illustrations of scenes from *Persuasion*.

35. An eighteenth-century village scene. All of Jane's novels are set in country villages such as this one.

Above left: 36. All of Jane's novels are love stories with a domestic setting.
Above right: 37. Card playing was popular in the Georgian period. There are many references to card games in Jane's novels and letters.

Above left: 38. The parlour in Chawton Cottage, with Jane's writing desk.
Above right: 39. Tea drinking was a popular social habit in Georgian England. Jane was in charge of the tea supplies at Chawton Cottage.
Left: 40. Chawton House, part of the Hampshire estates inherited by Edward Austen.

Above left: 41. The Oak Room, Chawton House.
Above right: 42. A copy of a letter from Jane to her niece Anna, written at Chawton Cottage in 1815.

43. Chawton House Museum, formerly Chawton Cottage. (Courtesy of Mariana Beadsworth)

Above: 44. Chawton House, Hampshire, unchanged since it was inherited by Jane's brother Edward from the Knight family in 1797.

Left: 45. Inscription on the front wall of Chawton House Museum. (Courtesy of Mariana Beadsworth)

Below left: 46. Chawton House Museum, a side view. (Courtesy of Mariana Beadsworth)

Above: 47. The graves of Mrs Austen and Cassandra Austen, in the graveyard of St Nicholas church, Chawton. (Courtesy of Mariana Beadsworth)

Right: 48. The church of St Nicholas, Chawton, Hampshire where Jane's brother Henry was curate from 1816-1820. (Courtesy of Mariana Beadsworth)

Below right: 49. Cottages in the village of Chawton. (Courtesy of Mariana Beadsworth)

Above left: 50. 8 College Street, Winchester, where Jane spent the last two months of her life and where she died on 18 July 1817. (Courtesy of Robin Amy)

Above right: 51. Jane's grave in Winchester Cathedral. (Courtesy of Robin Amy)

Left: 52. The memorial to Jane near her grave in Winchester Cathedral. (Courtesy of Robin Amy)

Friends imagined Jane and her mother setting off for their new life in Bath. 'We can fancy Mrs Austen and Jane in their post-chaise, taking a last glance at the parsonage, amidst its cowslip-decked meadows and its tall branching elms and sycamores, and then driving through the village and along the familiar lanes till, by the "Deane Gate", they entered the great western road which was to lead them far from their country life to Bath and the "busy hum of men".'[4]

On her arrival in Bath Jane wrote to Cassandra describing the journey from Hampshire. The letter was written from the home of the Leigh-Perrots at 1 Paragon, where Jane and her mother stayed while they looked for a home of their own.

> Our journey here was perfectly free from accident or Event; we changed Horses at the end of every stage, & paid at almost every Turnpike; – we had charming weather, hardly any Dust, & were exceedingly agreable (*sic*), as we did not speak above once in three miles. – Between Luggershall & Everley we made our grand meal, and then with admiring astonishment perceived in what a magnificent manner our support had been provided for; – We could not with the utmost exertion consume above the twentieth part of the beef … We had a very neat chaise from Devizes; it looked almost as well as a Gentleman's, at least as a very shabby Gentleman's–; inspite (*sic*) of this advantage however We were above three hours coming from thence to Paragon, & it was half way after seven by *Your* Clocks before we entered the house. Frank, whose black head was in waiting in the Hall window, received us very kindly; and his Master & Mistress did not shew less cordiality. – They both look very well, tho' my Aunt has a violent cough. We drank tea as soon as we arrived, & so ends the account of our Journey, which my Mother bore without fatigue.[5]

Later in the letter, Jane described her first disappointing impression of Bath: 'The first view (*sic*) of Bath in fine weather does not answer my expectations; I think I see more distinctly thro' Rain. – The sun was got behind everything, and the appearance of the place from the top of Kingsdown, was all vapour, shadow, smoke & confusion.'[6]

It was not long before Jane became involved in the busy life of Bath. She often accompanied her uncle on his morning walk to take the waters. Constance Hill imagined Jane and her uncle among the throngs of fashionably dressed people in the Pump Room, which she described as 'a dignified stone edifice, its four tall fluted pillars crowned with Corinthian capitals, supporting a sculpted pediment … a stone balustrade fronts an alcove in which the waters, rising in a marble basin, throw up a column of steam, and where the attendants in mob-caps and aprons, are busy filling and handing out glasses to the company'.[7]

Jane also attended a number of social events in the Assembly Rooms. The contemporary writer Pierce Egan described the grand ballroom, in the Upper Assembly Rooms, in the following words: 'The elegance of the ball room (which is 100 feet in length) astonishes every spectator. The ceiling is beautifully ornamented with panels having open compartments from which are suspended five superb glass chandeliers. The walls are painted and decorated in the most tasteful style; and the Corinthian columns and entablature resemble statuary marble. At each end of the room are placed, in magnificent gilt frames, the most splendid looking-glasses that could be procured to give effect to the general brilliant appearance.'[8]

Jane described one event held here in a letter to her sister, dated 12 to 13 May 1801.

In the evening I hope you honoured my Toilette & Ball with a thought; I dressed myself as well as I could, & had all my finery much admired at home. By nine o'clock my Uncle, Aunt & I entered the rooms & linked Miss Winstone on to us. – Before tea, it was rather a dull affair; but then the beforetea did not last long, for there was only one dance, danced by four couple. –Think of four couple, surrounded by about an hundred people, dancing in the upper rooms at Bath! – After tea we *cheered up*; the breaking up of private parties sent some scores more to the Ball, & tho' it was shockingly & inhumanly thin for this place, there were people enough I suppose to have made five or six very pretty Basingstoke assemblies.[9]

A description of the social gathering Jane was present at on the following night reveals how these occasions sometimes bored her. She relieved the boredom by scrutinising and judging her fellow guests.

Another stupid party last night; perhaps if larger they might be less intolerable, but here there were only just enough to make one card table, with six people to look over, & talk nonsense to each other. Ly Fust, Mrs Busby, & a Mrs Owen sat down with my Uncle to Whist within five minutes after the three old Toughs came in, & there they sat, with only the exchange of Adm: Stanhope for my Uncle, till their Chairs were announced. –I cannot anyhow continue to find people agreable (*sic*); I respect Mrs Chamberlayne for doing her hair well, but cannot feel a more tender sentiment. – Miss Langley is like any other short girl, with a broad nose & wide mouth, fashionable dress, & exposed bosom. –Adm: Stanhope is a gentleman-like Man, but then his legs are too short, & his tail too long.[10]

Life improved for Jane at the end of May, when her father and sister arrived in Bath. The four Austens moved into their new home, which was close to Sydney Gardens as Jane had wished. Constance Hill's description of the house, written at the beginning of the twentieth century, provides some idea of how it may well have looked when Jane lived there.

We have visited the house in Sydney Place, and have sat in the pretty drawing-room with its three tall windows overlooking the Gardens. The morning sun was streaming in at these windows and falling upon the quaint empire furniture which adorns the room, and which pleasantly suggests the Austens' sojourn there. The house is roomy and commodious. Beneath the drawing-room, which is on the first floor, are the dining-room and arched hall from which a passage leads to a garden at the back of the house. The large, old-fashioned kitchen, with its shining copper pans and its dresser, laden with fine old china, looked as if it had remained untouched since the Austens' day.[11]

Despite the fulfilment of her wish to live near Sydney Gardens, Jane must often have longed for the peace and tranquillity of the Hampshire countryside, especially on gala night. On these occasions the gardens thronged with visitors enjoying the music, singing, fireworks and colourful illuminations which made one contemporary writer liken them to the famous Vauxhall pleasure gardens in London. Jane and Cassandra probably found the gardens more to their taste during the day, when they could enjoy the labyrinth, the lawns, the woodland walks and the peaceful waters of the nearby Kennet and Avon Canal. Jane, no doubt, enjoyed all the pleasures which Bath had to offer much more with her sister by her side. The following contemporary description of a busy street in Bath, written by Pierce Egan, gives an impression of the fashionable city which was Jane's new home.

Milsom Street is the very magnet of Bath, the centre of attraction and, till the hour of dinner-time, the peculiar resort of the beau monde – where the familiar nod and the 'how do you do' are repeated fifty times in the course of the morning. All is bustle and gaiety, numerous dashing equipages passing and repassing, others gracing the doors of the tradesmen; sprinkled here and there with the invalids in the comfortable sedans and easy two-wheeled carriages. The shops are capacious and elegant. Among them the visitors find libraries to improve the mind, musical repositories to enrich their taste and science, confectioners to invite the most fastidious appetite, and tailors, milliners, & c. of the highest eminence in the fashionable world, to adorn the male and decorate and beautify the female, so as to render the form almost of statuary excellence.[12]

Although Jane did her best to enjoy all that Bath had to offer, the contrast with her former life could not have been greater.

Soon after moving into their new home, the Reverend and Mrs Austen took their daughters away for a holiday in Devon, probably to Sidmouth and Colyton. Details of this holiday are sketchy because, as the sisters were together, no letters were written describing it. It was probably while on this holiday that Jane met a man with whom she had a brief holiday romance. This romance remained a secret until, many years after Jane's death, her sister spoke about it to her niece Caroline. The details were related by Edward Austen-Leigh in his biography.

> She (Cassandra) said that, while staying at some seaside place, they became acquainted with a gentleman, whose charm of person, mind and manners was such that Cassandra thought him worthy to possess and likely to win her sister's love. When they parted, he expressed his intention of soon seeing them again; and Cassandra felt no doubt as to his motives. But they never again met. Within a short time they heard of his sudden death. I believe that, if Jane ever loved, it was this unnamed gentleman; but the acquaintance had been short, and I am unable to say whether her feelings were of such a nature as to affect her happiness.[13]

Caroline Austen considered that her aunt's attachment had not 'overclouded her happiness for long' as it 'had not gone far enough to leave misery behind'. If, however, Jane did grieve over the death of this 'unnamed gentleman', and the end of any hopes of marriage which the romance may have occasioned, she was no doubt comforted by her sister. As Cassandra's own romance had been ended abruptly by the death of her fiancé, she would have known how best to support Jane in similar circumstances.

Little detail is known about Jane's activities from the summer of 1801 until September 1804, because of a gap in her surviving correspondence. Unfortunately, information from other sources is incomplete. It is recorded that, in April 1802, James, Mary and Anna Austen visited their family in Bath. This visit may well have been awkward for Jane, because her relationship with her sister-in-law Mary had become strained by this time. There was a suspicion that it was Mary who first suggested that her father-in-law should retire, so that her husband could take over the living of Steventon. If there was any truth in this suspicion, it could account for the strained relationship. Jane, however, would have been pleased to see her brother, and delighted to be reunited with her niece. In later life Anna remembered this visit and recorded that her grandparents, to whom she was very attached, 'seemed to enjoy the cheerfulness of their Town life, and especially perhaps the rest which their advancing years entitled them to, which, even to their active natures, must have been acceptable...'[14]

Anna also recorded the following memory of her still handsome grandfather: 'My Grand Father as a young man was considered extremely handsome – so I have been told, and he was still handsome when advanced in age – At the time when I have the most perfect recollection of him he must have been getting on hard, as people say, for seventy. His hair in its whiteness might have belonged to a much older man; it was very beautiful &

glossy, with short curls above the ears ... I can well remember at Bath, where my Grand Father latterly resided, what notice he attracted, when on any public occasion he appeared with his head uncovered.'[15] Unfortunately Anna did not leave any description of her aunt Jane at this time.

In the summer of 1802 Charles Austen joined his parents and sisters on their holiday in Devon. It is also believed they went on to Wales. Jane and Cassandra were very fond of Charles, whom they called 'our own particular little brother', borrowing the description of a character in the novel *Camilla* by Fanny Burney.

The Austen sisters, accompanied by Charles, spent the autumn of 1802 paying brief visits to the James Austens at Steventon, and a longer one to the Edward Austens at Godmersham. Jane and Cassandra then went on to Manydown House, near Basingstoke, to stay with their friends Alethea and Catherine Bigg. It was during this visit that Jane received her only known offer of marriage. This unexpected proposal came from her friend's younger brother Harris Bigg-Wither, who was the heir to a considerable estate. Jane initially accepted this offer, but had second thoughts overnight and withdrew her acceptance the following morning. Jane was so distressed that she and Cassandra hurriedly left Manydown House and returned to Steventon Rectory. Much to the surprise of James and Mary Austen the sisters insisted, without explanation, that their brother accompany them back to Bath the next day. The family only found out later the reason for Jane's distress and the hasty retreat from Hampshire. In his biography Edward Austen-Leigh referred to this incident in the following words: 'In her youth she had declined the addresses of a gentleman who had the recommendations of good character, and connections, and position in life, of everything, in fact, except the subtle power of touching her heart.'[16]

Caroline Austen wrote of this affair, 'To be sure she should not have said yes – over night – but I have always respected her for the courage in cancelling that yes – the next morning – All worldly advantages would have been to her – & she was of an age to know *this* quite well – My Aunts had very small fortunes & on their Father's death they & their Mother would be, they were aware, but poorly off – I believe most young women so circumstanced would have taken Mr W. & trusted to love after marriage.'[17]

Jane was briefly tempted by the material, and other advantages, which marriage to Harris Bigg-Wither would have provided. However, despite the limitations on her life resulting from financial dependence on her father, Jane quickly realised that she could not marry a man she did not love. Mary Austen reputedly disapproved of Jane's rejection of such an eligible young man, but it is inconceivable that any other member of her family would have wished Jane to risk her happiness by marrying without love. Fortunately, Jane's long-standing friendship with Alethea and Catherine Bigg was not spoiled by her rejection of their brother.

6

BATH
1803–1805

During the winter of 1802 to 1803 Jane revised the manuscript of her novel *Susan*, with a view to getting it published. Jane had not originally intended to publish her novels. She possibly changed her mind because of the realisation that her chances of finding a man she loved enough to marry were diminishing, and that her best chance of achieving some financial independence lay in becoming a published writer. Early in 1803 the manuscript of *Susan* was sold to the London publisher Richard Crosby for £10. Henry Austen's business associate dealt with the publisher and stipulated that the work be published soon. Although Crosby did advertise its forthcoming publication, the novel was, for some unknown reason, never published. Much to Jane's disappointment her manuscript was filed away in the publisher's office, where it was to remain for many years.

The Austen family suffered a period of anxiety in the spring of this year, concerning Jane's brother Henry and his wife. Henry had, by this time, resigned his army commission and set himself up as a banker in London. Following the Peace of Amiens, signed in March 1802, hostilities had ended between Great Britain and France. Henry and Eliza Austen decided this would be a good time to travel to France, and try to recover the confiscated property of Eliza's first husband. While they were in France, Napoleon broke the terms of the peace treaty. Hostilities were resumed and orders were issued for the detention of all British nationals. Henry and Eliza only managed to escape arrest and internment in France because Eliza's excellent French enabled them to pass as a French couple.

The renewal of war resulted in both of Jane's sailor brothers being recalled to active service. Charles rejoined the *Endymion* as first lieutenant, where he remained until promotion in October 1804 to commander of HMS *Indian*. Frank, meanwhile, moved to Ramsgate in Kent to lead the Sea Fencibles, a unit set up to defend the coast against the threat of invasion. Jane must have visited Frank in Ramsgate in 1803 because Egerton Brydges, the brother of her friend Anne Lefroy, met her there. In later life he recalled this meeting and wrote this description of Jane's appearance: 'When I knew Jane Austen, I never suspected that she was an authoress: but my eyes told me that she was fair and handsome, slight and elegant, but with cheeks a little too full. The last time I think that I saw her was at Ramsgate in 1803; perhaps she was then about twenty-seven years old.'[1]

In the autumn of 1803 Jane left Bath to pay visits to Edward and his family at Godmersham, and the Lefroys at Ashe. In November she went to Lyme Regis in Dorset with her parents. This was her first visit to the seaside resort that was to provide the setting for part of her novel *Persuasion*.

Around this time Jane started to write another novel named *The Watsons*, but she did not complete it. The reason for this, according to Mary Augusta Austen-Leigh, was 'apparently because the author ceased to feel any interest in its contents'.[2] William and Richard Austen-Leigh observed that this unfinished manuscript was written in her beautiful handwriting on 'sheets which could be easily covered with a piece of blotting paper in case of the arrival of unexpected visitors, and which would thus fit in with her desire for secrecy'.[3]

There are several possible explanations for Jane's inability to compose any new writing during the years she spent in Bath. Mary Augusta Austen-Leigh suggested that the losses suffered when she left Hampshire had caused the creative muse to desert Jane during this period. 'She had lost her youth. At the age of twenty-five, while still a young woman, she had left her native place, her earliest friends, and every well-loved scene associated with the first overflowings of her happy girlish fancies. It was the birthplace, not of herself alone, but of many creations, born to a far longer existence than hers was destined to be upon earth – all those characters who live and move for us throughout the pages of her first three novels.'[4]

Unhappiness over the death of the man she met in Devon may have been another contributory factor. Nevertheless, Jane continued to collect material during this period, which she later used in her writing. She constantly observed the people around her, noting mannerisms, expressions and conversations. In the words of William and Richard Austen-Leigh, Bath 'had given her many opportunities of studying the particular types (of people) which she blended into her own creations'.[5] Jane also improved her knowledge of the topography and architecture of Bath, and soaked up its atmosphere so that she could use it as a setting for future novels.

In 1804 Henry and Eliza Austen accompanied his parents and sisters on their summer holiday to Devon and Dorset. They stayed in a cottage on a grassy hillside near the harbour. Many years later two of Jane's descendants went to Lyme to trace the places she visited on this holiday. They wrote the following description of the cottage they stayed in, unaware that it was the very one in which Jane herself had stayed:

…the house was nothing but a queer, ramshackle cottage with low rooms and small windows, and a staircase so narrow and steep and twisted, and withal dark, that it was a source of danger to get up and down it. Then there were two ground floor rooms, one in its proper place, containing kitchen, entrance and dining room, and the other at the top of the house, containing the bedrooms and back door, which latter opened on to the green hill behind. The drawing-room which, by comparison with the rest, might be called spacious, was on the middle floor, and from thence we had a charming view of the sea and harbour and Cobb, on one side, and of the pretty chain of eastern cliffs, on the other.[6]

Lyme Regis, with its steep main street straight down to the sea, quaint houses and the famous stone pier known as the Cobb, was the setting for some memorable scenes in *Persuasion*. Jane visited the nearby pretty villages of Charmouth, Uplyme and Pinny, which also feature in this novel. It was while on this holiday that Cassandra made a watercolour sketch of Jane, showing a back view of her sitting outside on a sunny day with the strings of her bonnet hanging loose.

Following this holiday the Austens moved into a new home in Bath at 3 Green Park Buildings. It was here that the news reached Jane in December of the death of her dear friend Anne Lefroy of Ashe, as a result of a fall from her horse after it bolted. This accident occurred on 16 December, Jane's twenty-ninth birthday. There is no record of how Jane reacted to this tragedy at the time, but a poem she wrote in memory of her friend, on the fourth anniversary of her death, reveals how deeply this loss affected her. This poem, which ran to eleven verses, opened with the following lines.

The day returns again, my natal day;
What mix'd emotions in my mind arise!

Beloved Friend, four years have passed away
Since thou were snatched for ever from our eyes.
The day commemorative of my birth,
Bestowing life, and light, and hope to me,
Brings back the hour which was thy last on earth,
O! bitter pang of torturing memory![7]

Early in the new year of 1805 Jane suffered an even more grievous loss, when her beloved father died. Although he had not been in the best of health, the death of George Austen was both sudden and unexpected. Jane sent the following letter containing the sad news to her brother Frank, who was on board HMS *Leopard* at Dungeness.

Monday 21st January 1805
Green Park Bgs
My dearest Frank,
I have melancholy news to relate, & sincerely feel for your feelings under the shock of it. –I wish I could better prepare You for it. – But having said so much, Your mind will already forestall the sort of Event which I have to communicate. – Our dear Father has closed his virtuous & happy life, in a death almost as free from suffering as his Children could have wished. He was taken ill on Saturday morning, exactly in the same way as heretofore, an oppression in the head with fever, violent tremulousness, & the greatest degree of Feebleness. The same remedy of Cupping, which had before been so successful, was immediately applied to– but without such happy effects. The attack was more violent, & at first he seemed scarcely at all releived (*sic*) by the Operation. – Towards the Evening however he got better, had a tolerable night, & yesterday morning was so greatly amended as to get up & join us at breakfast as usual, walk about with only the help of a stick, & every symptom was then so favourable that when

Bowen saw him at one, he felt sure of his doing perfectly well.
– But as the day advanced, all these comfortable appearances
gradually changed; the fever grew stronger than ever, & when
Bowen saw him at ten at night, he pronounc'd his situation to
be most alarming. – At nine this morning he came again – & by
his desire a Physician was called; – Dr Gibbs – But it was then
absolutely a lost case – Dr Gibbs said that nothing but a Miracle
could save him, and about twenty minutes after Ten he drew
his last gasp. – Heavy as is the blow, we can already feel that a
thousand comforts remain to us to soften it. Next to that of the
consciousness of his worth & constant preparation for another
World, is the remembrance of his having suffered, comparatively
speaking, nothing. – Being quite insensible of his own state, he
was spared all the pain of separation, & he went off almost in his
Sleep – My Mother bears the Shock as well as possible; she was
quite prepared for it, & feels all the blessing of his being spared
a long Illness. My Uncle and Aunt have been with us, & shew us
every imaginable kindness. And tomorrow we shall I dare say
have the comfort of James's presence, as an Express has been sent
to him. – We write also of course to Godmersham and Brompton.
Adieu my dearest Frank. The loss of such a Parent must be felt,
or we should be Brutes. – I wish I could have given you better
preparation – but it has been impossible.

Yous Ever Affecly

J. A.[8]

A second letter had to be sent to Frank the next day, as his ship
had moved on to Portsmouth before he could have received the
first one. The later letter contained a few additional sentences,
including the following: 'His tenderness as a Father, who can
do justice to? The serenity of his Corpse is most delightful
– it preserves the sweet, benevolent Smile which always
distinguished him.'[9]

George Austen was buried in the crypt of Walcot church in Bath, where he was married in 1764, under a tablet bearing the inscription; 'Under this stone rest the remains of the Rev. George Austen Rector of Steventon and Deane in Hampshire, who departed this life the 21st of January 1805, aged 73 years.'

Jane, who had always been closer to her father than her mother, felt her loss deeply. She was helped, however, by her strong religious faith and her belief that she would one day be reunited with him.

Following the death of George Austen, his widow and daughters found themselves in precarious financial circumstances. They moved several times in search of cheaper accommodation in Bath. Each of Jane's brothers, except Charles, generously pledged an annual sum, according to their means, to support their mother and sisters. Cassandra had a small income from the capital she had inherited from her fiancé, but Jane had no money of her own. Jane felt guilty about depending on her brothers, three of whom already had families to support. Unfortunately, financial dependence was the lot of the majority of women in Georgian England.

7

FROM BATH TO SOUTHAMPTON
1805–1809

In March 1805 Jane moved with her mother and sister to 25 Gay Street, Bath. Two chatty and amusing letters written in April to Cassandra, who was staying with the Lloyds at Ibthorpe, show that Jane's spirits were recovering after the loss of her father, and she was enjoying a busy social life once more. The next month the Austen sisters' friend Martha Lloyd joined their household following the death of her mother.

In the early summer the Austen ladies travelled to Godmersham, stopping on their way to collect Anna from Steventon. This visit was mentioned in the diary of Jane's niece Fanny. This diary is an interesting source of information about Jane from 1805 until her death. Fanny recorded the arrival of 'Grandmama Austen, Aunts Cassandra and Jane, and Anna' on Wednesday 19 June. Two days later she wrote of the birth at Steventon of James and Mary's daughter Caroline Mary Craven Austen, a younger sister for Edward and a half-sister for Anna.

Two diary entries describe 'a most delightful day' when Jane clearly enjoyed the pleasures of being an aunt.

Tuesday 25th June

We had a whole holiday. Aunts & Gmama played at school with us. Aunt C. was Miss Teachum, the Governess, Aunt Jane was Miss Popham, the teacher, Aunt Harriot, Sally the Housemaid, Miss Sharpe, the Dancing Master, the Apothecary & the Sergeant, Grandmama, Betty Jones the Pie Woman & Mama the Bathing Woman. They dressed in character & we had a most delightful day – After dessert we acted a Play called *Virtue Rewarded*. Anna was Duchess St Albans, I was the Fairy Serena & Fanny Cage a shepherdess Mona. We had a Bowl of Syllabub in the evening.

Tuesday 30th July

Aunts C. & Jane, Anna, Edward, George, Henry, William & myself acted *The Spoilt Child* & *Innocence Rewarded*, afterwards we danced & had a most delightful evening.

Miss Sharp, Fanny's governess, who was mentioned in the earlier entry, became a close friend and confidante of Jane's, and remained so until the end of Jane's life.

According to her niece's diary, Jane was fully occupied during her visit. She dined out with her brother and sister-in-law on a number of occasions and also went on trips to Canterbury, where she attended a ball on two consecutive evenings. Jane also met several members of Elizabeth Austen's family, including her brother Edward Bridges. Edward was very attentive towards Jane, and some light-hearted references to him in letters to her sister give the impression that he may have proposed to her, or at least attempted to.

In September Jane went to Sussex, as Fanny recorded in her diary for Tuesday 16.

Papa, Mama, Aunts C.& Jane & I set off from Godmersham for Battel (*sic*), where we arrived about 4, & finding no accommodation, we proceeded to Horsebridge where we slept.

We saw the abbey at Battel.

Wednesday 17th

We proceeded for Worthing, spent 2 or 3 hours at Brighton & arrived there at 5. We walked on the Sands in the evening.

Friday 19th

We dined at 4 & went to a Raffle in the evening, which Aunt Jane won & it amounted to 17s.

Fanny described the long walks and 'delicious dips in the sea' that she enjoyed before her return to Godmersham, leaving her aunts behind. Mrs Austen and Martha joined Cassandra and Jane in Worthing, where they remained until November. While they were enjoying this holiday the Battle of Trafalgar was fought. Reference to this epic victory was hidden amongst family news in Fanny's diary, sixteen days after it happened. 'Thursday 7th November. We heard of a very great Victory we had obtained over the French, but that Lord Nelson was killed.'

Jane's brother Frank, who had been recognised by Nelson as 'an excellent young man', had hoped to be put in command of a frigate under the great admiral. Much to his disappointment, however, Frank was involved in the Blockade of Cadiz and other duties when the Battle of Trafalgar took place and, therefore, had no share in the glory.

In January 1806 Mrs Austen moved her household to Trim Street in Bath; this was to be Jane's last home in that city. A few weeks later Frank Austen's involvement in the important victory over the French at San Domingo compensated for his disappointment at missing the Battle of Trafalgar. He was rewarded for his part in this victory with a gold medal and a silver vase. Jane, who was always proud of the achievements of her sailor brothers, was delighted for him. Frank, who had been engaged for some time to Mary Gibson, whom he had met at Ramsgate, was now in a secure enough financial position to plan his wedding. Mary became one of the best loved of Jane's sisters-in-law.

Around this time Jane's financial situation was improved, when she received a bequest of £50 in the will of a friend of her aunt Jane Leigh-Perrot. This was a considerable sum for Jane and was used to cover her personal expenses for the next year. Financial considerations were also behind Mrs Austen's determination to move away from the expensive city of Bath as soon as possible. She gladly accepted the offer of combining her household with that of Frank and Mary after their wedding, which was due to take place in July. The plan was to find lodgings in Southampton, which was a pleasant and fashionable location, as well as being convenient for Frank, who needed to be near Portsmouth.

On 2 July 1806 Mrs Austen, her daughters and Martha finally left Bath, an event which led to 'happy feelings of escape'[1] in Jane. Although she had enjoyed some aspects of life in Bath, this had been an unsettled and creatively inactive period for her, and she had never really felt at home there. Before leaving Bath Jane wrote a neat copy of the manuscript of *Lady Susan* and added a conclusion. This was the only satisfactory writing she achieved during this period, but she had accumulated a valuable store of impressions and memories to use in the future.

In the summer of 1806 Jane accompanied her mother on a series of visits to relatives. Their first stop was Adlestrop rectory in Gloucestershire, the home of the Reverend Thomas Leigh, a cousin of Mrs Austen. In early August Thomas Leigh took his guests to Stoneleigh Abbey in Warwickshire, which he had recently inherited. Stoneleigh Abbey, originally a Cistercian monastery founded in 1155, came into the possession of the Leigh family after the dissolution of the monasteries. King Charles I stayed there on his way to Nottinghamshire at the start of the Civil War. With her great interest in history and sympathy for the royal house of Stuart, Jane must have found the abbey a fascinating place to stay. Mrs Austen wrote a letter to her daughter-in-law in Steventon describing this visit.

> And here we all found ourselves on Tuesday (that is yesterday sennight) Eating Fish, venison & all manner of good things, at a late hour, in a Noble large Parlour, hung round with family Pictures– every thing is very Grand & very fine & very Large ... I expected to find everything about the place very fine & all that, but I had no idea of its being so beautiful, I had figured to myself long Avenues, dark rookeries & dismal Yew Trees, but there are no such melancholy things; The Avon runs near the house, amidst Green Meadows, bounding (*sic*) by large and beautiful Woods, full of delightful Walks ... We walk a good deal, for the woods are impenetrable to the sun, even in the middle of an August day. I do not fail to spend some part of every day in the kitchen garden, where the quantity of small fruit exceeds anything you can form an idea of ... Our visit has been a most pleasant one. We all seem in good humour, disposed to be pleased, and endeavouring to be agreeable, and I hope we succeed. Poor Lady Saye and Sele (a relative), to be sure, is rather tormenting, though sometimes amusing, and affords Jane many a good laugh, but she fatigues me sadly on the whole.[2]

This summer concluded with a five-week stay with Edward Cooper and his family in Staffordshire, where Jane was unfortunate enough to catch whooping cough from his children. In October Mrs Austen and Jane moved into temporary lodgings in Southampton, with the recently married Frank and Mary. Jane was in low spirits for a while, but her depression lifted when the household moved into a permanent home in Castle Square, with wide-ranging views of the Solent. The house belonged to Lord Lansdowne. Edward Austen-Leigh remembered visiting this house as a child, and wrote the following description of it: 'My grandmother's house had a pleasant garden, bounded on one side by the old city walls;

the top of this wall was sufficiently wide to afford a pleasant walk, with an extensive view, easily accessible to ladies by steps.'[3]

Jane described the garden of their new home, which was the envy of their neighbours, in a letter to her sister, who was away when the move to Castle Square took place.

Our Garden is putting in order, by a Man who bears a remarkably good character, has a very fine complexion & asks something less than the first. The shrubs which border the gravel walk he says are only sweetbriar & roses, & the latter of an indifferent sort;– we mean to get a few of a better kind therefore, & at my own particular desire he procures us some Syringas. I could not do without a Syringa, for the sake of Cowper's Line. –We talk also of a Laburnum – The Border under the Terrace Wall, is clearing away to receive Currants & Gooseberry Bushes, & a spot is found very proper for Raspberries.[4]

Jane also described the improvements being made to the house. 'The alterations & improvements within doors too advance very properly, & the Offices will be made very convenient indeed. – Our Dressing-Table is constructing on the spot, out of a large Kitchen Table belonging to the House, for doing which we have the permission of Mr Husket Lord Landown's Painter, – domestic Painter I shd call him, for he lives in the Castle – Domestic Chaplains have given way to this more necessary office, & I suppose whenever the Walls want no touching up, he is employed about my Lady's face.'[5]

William and Richard Austen-Leigh noted that 'they were living in a very quiet way, not caring to add to their acquaintance more than was necessary … The Austens were near enough to Steventon to be visited occasionally by James Austen and his wife, and between their own acquaintance, and Frank's friends in the service, they had what they wanted in the way of society.'[6]

Jane described some of her new acquaintances in letters to her sister. The following extract is from a letter dated 7–8 January 1807:

To the Berties are to be added the Lances, with whose cards we have been endowed, and whose visit Frank and I returned yesterday. They live about a mile and three-quarters from S. to the right of the new road to Portsmouth, and I believe their house is one of those which are to be seen almost anywhere among the woods on the other side of the Itchen. It is a handsome building, stands high, and in a very beautiful situation. We found only Mrs Lance at home, and whether she boasts any offspring besides a grand pianoforte did not appear. She was civil and chatty enough, and offered to introduce us to some acquaintance in Southampton, which we gratefully declined. I suppose they must be acting by the orders of Mr Lance of Netherton in this civility, as there seems no other reason for their coming near us. They will not come often, I dare say. They live in a handsome style and are rich, and she seemed to like to be rich, and we gave her to understand that we were far from being so; she will soon feel therefore, that we are not worth her acquaintance.[7]

In her next letter Jane described a visit from the daughter of one of Frank's colleagues, which shows how much she delighted in the company of children.

The morning was so wet that I was afraid we should not be able to see our little Visitor, but Frank who alone could go to Church called for her after Service, & she is now talking away at my side, & examining the Treasures of my Writing-desk drawer; – very happy I beleive (*sic*); – not at all shy of course. – Her name is Catherine & her Sister's Caroline. – She is something like her Brother, & as short for her age, but not so well-looking. – What is become of all the Shyness in the World? … Our little Visitor has just left us, & left us highly pleased with her; – she is a nice, natural, open-hearted, affectionate girl, with all the ready civility which one sees in the best Children of the present day;- so unlike anything that I was myself at her age, that I am often all astonishment & shame. – Half her time here was spent at Spillikins; which I consider as a very valuable part of our Household furniture, & as not the least important Benefaction from the family of Knight to that of Austen.[8]

Frank Austen's naval career took him away to sea a great deal at this time, leaving his wife and baby daughter Mary Jane, born in April, with his mother and sisters. Jane's younger brother Charles, whose naval career was also proceeding well, married Fanny Palmer, daughter of the former Attorney General of Bermuda, in May 1807.

In September of this year Mrs Austen and her daughters joined a large family gathering at Chawton Great House, her son Edward's other residence. This was the first of many happy visits Jane was to make to the house, which was visited by Constance Hill and described in her biography of Jane: 'The house, a fine old Elizabethan mansion, with its Tudor porch, and its heavy mullioned windows, may be seen by the passer-by, standing on rising ground; while a little below it, in a gentle hollow, lies the old church of Chawton – a small grey stone edifice embowered in trees.'[9]

This was also young Fanny Austen's first visit to Chawton Great House, which had until recently been rented out to tenants. Fanny described the house in a letter to her former governess.

This is a fine large old house, built long before Queen Elizabeth I believe, & here are such a number of old irregular passages & c & c that it is very entertaining to explore them, & often when I think myself miles away from one part of the house I find a passage or entrance close to it, & I don't know when I shall be quite mistress of all the intricate and different ways. It is very curious to trace the genealogy of the Knights and all the old families that have possessed this estate, from the pictures of which there are quantities, & some descriptions of them have been routed out, so that we are not at a loss for amusement. There are quantities of Trees about the house (especially Beech) which always make a place pretty I think.[10]

In September Edward took his family to Southampton to stay with their Austen relatives. The following entries in Fanny's diary show Jane enjoying the pleasures of spending time with her family.

Sunday 13th September

We all went to Church & afterwards walked to the Polygon (an area of the city)

Monday 14th September

In the evening Papa, Aunts C & J, Wm.& I went to the play. They performed *The Way to Keep Him*.

Tuesday 15th September

We went in a hired boat to Hythe to call on Mrs Palmer (Charles Austen's mother-in-law) who called on us the day before. Mama, to everybody's astonishment, was of the party and not at all sick. In the evening Uncle Henry A came. Aunts C & J walked in the High Street till late.

Wednesday 16th September

We all, excepting Mama, took a boat and went to Netley Abbey, the ruins of which are beautiful. We eat there of some biscuits we had taken and returned quite delighted. Aunt Jane & I walked in the High Street till late.

The year 1808 was a busy one socially for Jane as she paid visits to, and received visits from, a number of relatives and friends. Early in the year Jane and her sister went to stay with the Fowles, the family of Cassandra's late fiancé Tom. Tom's brother Fulwar later remembered meeting Jane, and left the following description of her: 'She was pretty – certainly pretty – bright & a good deal of color (*sic*) in her face – like a doll – no that wd. not give at all the idea for she had so much expression – she was like a child – quite a child very lively & full of humor (*sic*) – most amiable – most beloved.'[11]

In May Jane went to London to stay with Henry and Eliza, who were then living at Brompton. Jane always enjoyed visiting London, not only because of her closeness to Henry and Eliza, but also because of the pleasures the capital had to offer. On this occasion she witnessed the ladies arriving at Court for the birthday celebrations of King George III.

A few weeks later James and Mary and their children collected Jane and took her with them to Godmersham. Jane wrote to Cassandra describing the warm welcome she received. This letter shows how important Edward and his family were to her, as well as her delight in, and attachment to, her nephews and nieces.

Our two brothers were walking before the house as we approached, as natural as life. Fanny and Lizzy met us in the Hall with a great deal of pleasant joy; we went for a few minutes into the breakfast parlour, and then proceeded to our rooms. Mary has the Hall chamber. I am in the Yellow room – very literally – for I am writing in it at this moment. It seems odd to me to have such a great place all to myself, and to be at Godmersham without you is also odd, You are wished for, I assure you: Fanny, who came to me as soon as she had seen her Aunt James to her room, and stayed while I dressed, was as energetic as usual in her longings for you. She is grown both in her height and size since last year, but not immoderately, looks very well and seems as to conduct and manner just what she was and what one could wish to continue. Elizabeth, who was dressing when we arrived, came to me for a minute attended by Marianne, Charles and Louisa, and, you will not doubt, gave me a very affectionate welcome. That I had received such from Edward also I need not mention; but I do, you see, because it is a pleasure.[12]

Jane particularly enjoyed the company of her eldest niece Fanny during this visit. They became so close that Jane told Cassandra that Fanny had become 'almost another sister', and that she 'could not have supposed that a niece would ever have been so much to me'.[13] The following extracts from Jane's letters give an idea of how she spent her time at Godmersham.

15th–17th June 1808

Yesterday passed quite a la Godmersham; the gentlemen rode about Edward's farm, and returned in time to saunter along Bentigh with us; and after dinner we visited the Temple Plantations, which, to be sure, is a Chevalier Bayard of a plantation. James and Mary are much struck with the beauty of the place. To-day the spirit of the thing is kept up by the two brothers being gone to Canterbury in the chair. I cannot discover, even through Fanny, that her mother is fatigued by her attendance on the children. I have, of course, tendered my services, and when Louisa (Elizabeth's sister) is gone, who sometimes hears the little girls read, will try to be accepted in her stead.[14]

30th June–1st July

Our Tuesday's Engagement went off very pleasantly; we called first on Mrs Knight, & found her very well; & at dinner had only the Milles of Nackington in addition to Goodnestone and Godmersham & Mrs Moore ... In the Eveng came Mr Moore, Mr

Toke, Dr & Mrs Walsby & others; – one Card Table was formed, the rest of us sat & talked, & at half after nine we came away.[15]

While in Kent, Jane spent a few days with Edward's adoptive mother Mrs Knight at her home in Canterbury. The wealthy Mrs Knight gave Jane 'a very agreeable present' of some money, which Jane told her sister would make her 'circumstances quite easy'.[16]

When she returned to Southampton in early July, after a happy stay at her brother's home, Jane had no idea that life at Godmersham was soon to change and would never be the same again. At the end of September 1808 Cassandra travelled to Kent to help her sister-in-law during the birth of her eleventh baby, a service she had performed many times before. On this occasion Cassandra arrived too late for the delivery on 28 September, but wrote to inform Jane that the mother and her newborn son, Brook John, were both well. Elizabeth continued to do well until 10 October, when she suddenly and unexpectedly died, as described in her daughter's diary entry for that day: 'Oh! The miserable events of this day! My mother, my beloved mother torn from us after eating a hearty dinner. She was taken violently ill and expired (God have mercy upon us) after 1/2 an hour!!!'

Jane's letter to Cassandra on receiving the sad news contained a short paragraph of praise for Elizabeth, and relief that she only suffered briefly before going 'from this world to a better'.[17] Jane's main concern, however, was for her widowed brother and his motherless children. She was particularly worried about Fanny who, as the eldest daughter, would now have to take on the heavy burden of running a large country house, care for her siblings, and support her father at the tender age of sixteen.

Edward's eldest sons, Edward and George, were at school in Winchester when their mother died. They were brought to Southampton to be comforted by their grandmother and Aunt

Jane. The latter occupied and distracted her nephews from their grief by playing games with them, and taking them out for walks and on a boat trip. She also arranged for a local tailor to fit them out with mourning clothes, because she 'would not have them made uncomfortable by the want of what is usual on such occasions'.[18] Cassandra stayed on at Godmersham for some months to support her brother, and help her niece to run the household.

In 1809 Frank Austen was fighting in the Peninsula War in Spain as commander of the *St Albans*. Jane kept herself informed of what was happening in this war, and of political events closer to home, as indicated by the following extract from a letter dated 10–11 January 1809: 'The *St Albans* perhaps may soon be off to help bring home what may remain by this time of our poor Army, whose state seems dreadfully critical. – The Regency seems to have been heard of only here, my most political Correspondants (*sic*) make no mention of it.'[19] While Frank was serving in the Peninsula War his brother Charles, who wrote to Jane regularly, was based in the West Indies.

Shortly after his wife's death, Edward offered his mother and sisters a new home, as related by his nephew in his biography. 'In 1809 Mr Knight was able to offer his mother the choice of two houses on his property; one near his usual residence at Godmersham Park in Kent; the other near Chawton House, his occasional residence in Hampshire. The latter was chosen...'[20]

Needless to say, Jane was delighted at the prospect of returning to her beloved north Hampshire. Her final weeks in Southampton were filled with social engagements and she informed Cassandra that 'everybody is very much concerned at our going away, & everybody is acquainted with Chawton & speaks of it as a remarkably pretty village; & everybody knows the House we describe – but nobody fixes on the right'.[21]

Jane seemed to be thinking once more about writing because

before leaving Southampton she wrote the following letter, under an assumed name, to Messrs Crosby & Son in an attempt to get them to publish her novel *Susan*.

Wednesday 5th April 1809.

Gentlemen,

In the Spring of 1803 a Ms. Novel in 2 vol. entitled *Susan* was sold to you by a Gentleman of the name of Seymour, & the purchase money £10. recd. at the same time. Six years have since passed, & this work of which I avow myself the Authoress, has never to the best of my knowledge, appeared in print, tho' an early publication was stipulated for at the time of the Sale. I can only account for such an extraordinary circumstance by supposing the MS by some carelessness to have been lost; & if that was the case, am willing to supply You with another Copy if you are disposed to avail yourselves of it, & will engage for no farther delay when it comes into your hands. – It will not be in my power from particular circumstances to command this Copy before the Month of August, but then, if you accept my proposal, you may depend on receiving it. Be so good as to send me a Line in answer, as soon as possible, as my stay in this place will not exceed a few days. Should no notice be taken of this Address, I shall feel myself at liberty to secure the publication of my work, by applying elsewhere. I am Gentlemen &c&c

M.A.D.

Direct to Mrs Ashton Dennis

Post Office, Southampton[22]

Jane received the following disappointing reply to her letter.

Saturday 8th April 1809

Madam,

We have to acknowledge the receipt of your letter of the 5th inst. It is true that at the time mentioned we purchased of Mr

Seymour a MS. novel entitled *Susan* and paid him for it the sum of 10£ for which we have his stamped receipt as a full consideration, but there was not any time stipulated for its publication, neither are we bound to publish it. Should you or anyone else we shall take proceedings to stop the sale. The MS. shall be yours for the same as we paid for it.

For R. Crosby & Co

I am yours etc.

Richard Crosby[23]

The reason why Crosby failed to publish this novel in 1803 is unknown. When Jane wrote prompting them to publish it, however, the Gothic novel which it parodied had gone out of fashion, and this may account for their refusal to do so then. As she did not have ten pounds with which to buy back her manuscript it remained in the possession of Richard Crosby.

On 7 July 1809 Mrs Austen, her daughters and Martha moved into their new home in the village of Chawton. This was the beginning of a happy period in Jane's life.

8

CHAWTON
1809–1810

The letters Jane wrote to her sister at the end of 1808 and the beginning of 1809 show how eagerly she looked forward to moving to Chawton. In her letter dated 27 to 28 December 1808 Jane wrote, 'Yes, yes, we *will* have a Pianoforte, as good a one as can be got for 30 Guineas – & I will practise country dances, that we may have some amusement for our nephews & neices (*sic*), when we have the pleasure of their company.'[1] Jane was delighted to hear from Cassandra that their young nephew William was 'working a footstool' for their new home.

On 7 July 1809 Mrs Austen, her daughters and Martha Lloyd moved into their new home. This was the beginning of a more settled and contented period in Jane's life, during which the creative muse returned to her and she wrote much of her most important literary work. In the words of Jane's nephew Edward, 'Chawton must also be considered the place most closely connected with her career as a writer; for there it was that, in the maturity of her mind, she either wrote or rearranged, and prepared for publication, the books by which she has become known to the world.'[2]

Constance Hill wrote the following description of Chawton, which had changed little in the hundred years since Jane moved there: 'The village of Chawton lies in a specially beautiful part of

Hampshire, about five miles from Gilbert White's own Selborne, and, like it, famed for its hop fields and its graceful "hangers"; while within easy reach is the cheerful little town of Alton.'[3]

There were nearly 400 people living in Chawton in 1809, many of whom worked on the land or in the nearby forests. Jane's new neighbours included the Reverend John Papillon, the rector, who lived close by with his sister, the Prowting family and Miss Benn, a poor spinster who lived alone in a dilapidated cottage.

Chawton Cottage was close enough to Steventon to enable James and his family to pay frequent visits, and was just a short walk away from Chawton Great House, where Edward and his children stayed from time to time. Henry Austen's bank had a branch in Alton, which meant that he could visit his mother and sisters whenever he was in the area on business. Frank Austen was in China at this time but his wife Mary, who gave birth to her second baby in July 1809, had recently moved into a cottage not far from Chawton. Mrs Austen and her daughters were now within easy reach of most of their family and old friends, such as the Bigg sisters, which added to Jane's new-found contentment.

Chawton Cottage was previously occupied by the steward of Edward's Chawton estate. Caroline Austen described the cottage and her memories of staying there in the following paragraphs:

I have been told I know not how truthfully, that it had been originally a roadside Inn – and it was well placed for such a purpose – just where the road from Winchester comes into the London and Gosport line – The fork between the two being partly occupied by a large shallow pond – which pond I beleive (*sic*) has long since become dry ground.

The front door opened on the road, a very narrow enclosure of each side protected the house from the possible shock of any runaway vehicle – A good-sized entrance, and two parlours called dining room and drawing room, made the length of the house; all intended originally to look on the road – but the large drawing room window was blocked-up and turned into a bookcase when Mrs Austen took possession and another was opened at the side, which gave to view only turf and trees – a high wooden fence shut out the road (the Winchester road it was) all the length of the little domain, and trees were planted inside to form a shrubbery walk – which carried round the enclosure, gave a very sufficient space for exercise – you did not feel cramped for room; and there was a pleasant irregular mixture of hedgerow, and grass, and gravel walk and long grass for mowing, and orchard – which I imagine arose from two or three little enclosures having been thrown together, and arranged as best might be, for ladies' occupation – There was besides a good kitchen garden, large court and many out-buildings, not much occupied – and all this affluence of space was very delightful to children and I have no doubt added considerably to the pleasure of a visit.[4]

Everything indoors and *out* was well kept – the house was well furnished, and it was altogether a comfortable and ladylike establishment, tho' I beleive (*sic*) the means which supported it were but small.

The house was quite as good as the generality of Parsonage houses then – and much in the same old style – the ceilings low and roughly finished – *some* bedrooms very small – *none* very large but in number sufficient to accomodate (*sic*) the inmates, and several guests.

The dining room could not be made to look anywhere but on the road – and there my grandmother often sat for an hour or two in the morning, with her work or her writing – cheered by its sunny aspect and by the stirring scene it afforded her.

I beleive (*sic*) the close vicinity of the road was really no more an evil to her than it was to her grandchildren. Collyer's daily coach with six horses was a sight to see! and most delightful was it to a child to have the awful stillness of night so frequently broken by the noise of passing carriages, which seemed sometimes, even to shake the bed.[5]

Anna recalled that Jane and Cassandra were responsible for the housekeeping at Chawton Cottage, while their mother 'found plenty of occupation for herself in gardening and needlework. The former was with her, no idle pastime, no mere cutting of roses and tying up of flowers. She dug up her own potatoes, and I have no doubt she planted them, for the kitchen garden was as much her delight as the flower borders, and I have heard my mother say that, when at work, she wore a green round frock like a day-labourer's.'[6]

Caroline Austen remembered Chawton Cottage as a happy and harmonious home, with plenty of visitors coming and going.

In the time of my childhood, it was a cheerful house – my Uncles – one or another, frequently coming for a few days; and they were all pleasant in their own family – I have thought since, after having seen more of other households, *wonderfully*, as the family talk had much of spirit and vivacity, and it was never troubled by disagreements as it was not their habit to argue with each other – There always was perfect harmony amongst the brothers and sisters, and over my Grandmother's door might have been inscribed the text, 'Behold how good – and joyful a thing it is, brethren, to dwell together in unity.' There was firm family union, never broken but by death...[7]

Caroline wrote the following description of how her aunt occupied her time at her new home:

Aunt Jane began her day with music – for which I conclude she had a natural taste; as she thus kept it up – tho' she had no one to teach; was never induced (as I have heard) to play in company; and none of her family cared much for it. I suppose, that she might not trouble them, she chose her practising time before breakfast – when she could have the room to herself – She practised regularly every morning – She played very pretty tunes, *I* thought – and I liked to stand by her and listen to them, but the music, (for I knew the books well in after years) would now be thought disgracefully easy – Much that she played from was manuscript, copied out by herself – and so neatly and correctly, that it was as easy to read as print.

At 9 o'clock she made breakfast – *that* was *her* part of the household work – The tea and sugar stores were under *her* charge – *and* the wine – Aunt Cassandra did all the rest – for my Grandmother had suffered herself to be superseded by her daughters *before* I can remember; and soon *after*, she ceased even to sit at the head of the table.

I don't beleive (*sic*) Aunt Jane observed any particular method in parcelling out her day but I think she generally sat in the drawing room till luncheon: when visitors were there, chiefly at work – She was fond of work – and she was a great adept at overcast and satin stitch – the peculiar delight of that day – General handiness and neatness were amongst her characteristics – She could throw the spilikens for us, better than anyone else, and she was wonderfully successful at cup and ball – She found a resource sometimes in that simple game, when she suffered from weak eyes and could not work or read for long together.

After luncheon, my Aunts generally walked out – sometimes they went to Alton for shopping – Often, one or the other of them, to the Great House – as it was then called – when a brother was inhabiting it, to make a visit – or if the house were standing empty they liked to stroll about the grounds – sometimes to Chawton Park – a noble beech wood, just within a walk – but sometimes, but that was rarely, to call on a neighbour – They had no carriage, and their visitings did not extend far – there were a few families living in the village – but no great intimacy was kept up with any of them – they were upon *friendly* but rather *distant* terms, with all – Yet I am sure my Aunt Jane had a regard for her neighbours and felt a kindly interest in their proceedings. She liked immensely to hear all about them.

I did not often see my Aunt with a book in her hand, but I beleive (*sic*) she was fond of reading and that she *had* read and *did* read a good deal.

My Aunt must have spent much time in writing – her desk lived in the drawing room. I often saw her writing letters on it, and I beleive (*sic*) she wrote much of her Novels in the same way – sitting with her family, when they were quite alone; but I never saw any manuscript of *that* sort, in progress – She wrote very fully to her Brothers when they were at sea, and she corresponded with many others of her family...[8]

Caroline Austen remembered that her aunt often sang songs to her own accompaniment on the piano. The song Jane sang most frequently was a 'little French ditty' which her niece often asked her to sing. Caroline also remembered hearing Jane reading aloud in her 'very good speaking voice', the tones of which 'have never been forgotten – I can recall them even now'.[9]

Probably the most important advantage of moving to Chawton was that Jane was able to start writing again. In the words of William and Richard Austen-Leigh, 'She was no doubt aided by the quiet of her home and its friendly surroundings. In this tranquil spot, where the past and present even now join peaceful hands, she found happy leisure, repose of mind, and absence of distraction, such as any sustained creative effort demands.'[10]

The Austen-Leighs observed that much had happened to Jane since her early writing period. 'Since her fit of youthful enthusiasm, when she had composed three stories in little more than three years, she had had much experience of life to sober and strengthen her. Three changes of residence, the loss of her father, the friendship of Mrs Lefroy and the shock of her death, her own and her sister's sad love stories, the crisis in the Leigh Perrot history, and her literary disappointments. All these must have made her take up her two old works with a chastened spirit, and a more mature judgement.'[11]

Edward Austen-Leigh remembered his aunt starting to write again when she moved to Chawton Cottage, 'but as soon as she was fixed in her second home, she resumed the habits of composition which had been formed in her first, and continued them to the end of her life. The first year of her residence at Chawton seems to have been devoted to revising and preparing for the press *Sense and Sensibility* and *Pride and Prejudice.*'[12]

Writing at Chawton Cottage was not easy for Jane, according to her nephew.

> For she had no separate study to retire to, and most of the work must have been done in the general sitting-room, subject to all kinds of casual interruptions. She was careful that her occupation should not be suspected by servants, or visitors, or any persons beyond her own family party. She wrote upon small sheets of paper which could easily be put away, or covered with a piece of blotting paper. There was, between the front door and the offices, a swing door which creaked when it was opened; but she objected to having this little inconvenience remedied, because it gave notice when anyone was coming.[13]

Around this time Jane was encouraged to find a publisher for the revised novel, now entitled *Sense and Sensibility*, as related by Henry Austen in his *Memoir of Miss Austen*. 'She became an authoress entirely from taste and inclination. Neither the hope of fame nor profit mixed with her early motives. It was with extreme difficulty that her friends, whose partiality she suspected, whilst she honoured their judgement, could persuade her to publish her first work.'[14]

In the winter of 1809 to 1810 the manuscript was accepted for publication, at the author's expense, by Thomas Egerton of Whitehall, London. Jane was so certain that she would not recover the expense of publication that she put aside a sum from her modest income to cover the expected loss. As Jane still wished to keep her novel writing a secret, the words 'by a lady' appeared in the place of her name on the title page.

Jane continued to take great pleasure in the company of her many nephews and nieces. They were a great source of enjoyment to her, and she was a source of much delight to them. Frank's second child, Francis-William, was born on 12 July 1809. His aunt Jane wrote some amusing verses, addressed to her brother, to commemorate the event, which began, 'My dearest Frank, I wish you joy / Of Mary's safety with a Boy / Whose birth has given little pain / Compared with that of Mary Jane.'

This poem, which looked back on some of the events of Frank's childhood, concluded with the following verse in praise of Jane's new home:

As for ourselves we're very well;
As unaffected prose will tell. –
Cassandra's pen will paint our state,
The many comforts that await
Our Chawton home, how much we find
Already in it, to our mind;
And how convinced, that when complete
It will all other Houses beat
That ever have been made or mended,
With rooms concise, or rooms distended.
You'll find us very snug next year

Perhaps with Charles & Fanny near,
For now it often does delight us,
To fancy them just over-right us.[15]

All three of James Austen's children had affectionate childhood memories of their aunt. In his *Memoir* Edward wrote, 'I have not forgotten that Aunt Jane was the delight of all her nephews and nieces. We did not think of her as being clever, still less as being famous; but we valued her as one always kind, sympathising and amusing.'[16]

Anna remembered how popular her aunt was with children. 'Aunt Jane was the general favourite with children; her ways with them being so playful, and her long circumstantial stories so delightful! These were continued from time to time, and were begged for on all possible and impossible occasions; woven, as she proceeded, out of nothing but her own happy talent for invention. Ah! if but one of them could be recovered!'[17]

Caroline recalled,

My visits to Chawton were frequent. I cannot tell *when* they began – they were very pleasant to me – and Aunt Jane was the great charm – As a very little girl, I was always creeping up to her, and following her whenever I could, in the house and out of it – I might not have remembered this, but for the recollection of my mother's telling me privately, I must not be troublesome to my aunt.

Her charm to children was great sweetness of manner – she seemed to love you, and you loved her naturally in return – *This* as well as I can now recollect and analyse, was what I felt in my earliest days, before I was old enough to be amused by her cleverness – But soon came the delight of her playful talk – *Every*thing she could make amusing to a child – Then, as I got older, and when cousins came to share the entertainment, she would tell us the most delightful stories chiefly of Fairyland, and her Fairies had all characters of their own – The tale was invented, I am sure, at the moment, and was sometimes continued for 2 or 3 days, if occasion served.[18]

Jane became a great support to her motherless nieces, Anna and Fanny, as they approached womanhood. In many ways she fulfilled a mother's role for them, by acting as their confidante and advisor. Fanny's diary notes the letters she wrote to, and received from, her aunt and shows how often she was in Fanny's thoughts. Fanny also recorded details in her diary of two long visits she made to Chawton with her father in 1809 and 1810, and described the activities she enjoyed with Jane, such as shopping in Alton.

According to William and Richard Austen-Leigh, both Fanny and Anna 'occupied a good deal of Jane's thoughts and affections; but Anna must have been the one who caused her the most amusement and also the most anxiety … She cherished an ardent affection for her Aunt Jane, who evidently exercised a great influence on her character.'[19]

The 'anxiety' caused by Anna was the result of a short-lived engagement to a young man, deemed unsuitable by her father and step-mother. Jane cheered Anna up, and helped her to deal with her unhappiness over this affair, by writing a witty poem entitled 'Mock Panegyric to a Young Friend'. This poem, which began 'In measured verse, I now rehearse the charms of lovely Anna', advised her sixteen-year-old niece on the dangers of not keeping her emotions in check. This was something which Jane had considered in depth, as it was a theme explored in her novel *Sense and Sensibility*.

Family memoirs contain a number of descriptions of Jane's appearance as an adult. This is fortunate, as the only picture of undisputed provenance (with the exception of the watercolour of her back view) which exists of Jane, is a sketch drawn by her sister around 1810, which was described by Anna as 'hideously unlike'.[20] Caroline Austen described her aunt's appearance in the following paragraphs:

> As to my Aunt's personal appearance, her's was the first face that I can remember thinking pretty, not that I used that word to myself, but I know I looked at her with admiration – Her face was rather round than long – she had a bright, but not a pink colour – a clear brown complexion and very good hazle (*sic*) eyes … Her hair, a darkish brown, curled naturally – it was in short curls round her face (for then ringlets were not). She always wore a cap – Such was the custom with ladies who were not quite young – at least of a morning but I never saw her without one, to the best of my remembrance, either morning or evening.
>
> I beleive (*sic*) my two Aunts were not accounted very good dressers, and were thought to have taken to the garb of middle age unnecessarily soon – but they were particularly neat, and they held all untidy ways in great disesteem.[21]

Edward Austen-Leigh wrote a similar description of his aunt's face and added that 'her figure was rather tall and slender, her step light and firm, and her whole appearance expressive of health and animation'.[22] Henry Austen noted that his sister's 'features were separately good' and that 'their assemblage produced an unrivalled expression of that cheerfulness, sensibility, and benevolence, which were her real characteristics'.[23]

Family memoirs contain some other interesting insights into Jane's character. She was remembered as being serious and intense, as well as light-hearted and fun-loving. Anna Austen described Jane's character and compared it to that of her sister: 'Her unusually quick sense of the ridiculous inclined her to play with the trifling commonplaces of every day life, whether as regarded people or things; but she never played with its serious duties or responsibilities – when grave she was *very* grave; I am not sure but that Aunt Cassandra's disposition was the most equably cheerful of the two.'[24]

Edward Austen-Leigh summed up the difference between his two aunts: 'They were not exactly alike. Cassandra's was the colder and calmer disposition; she was always prudent and well-judging, but with less outward demonstration of feeling and less sunniness of temper than Jane possessed.'[25]

Edward added that his aunt was 'as ready to comfort the unhappy or to nurse the sick as to laugh and jest with the light-hearted'.[26] Other characteristics remembered by Jane's family were her humility and modesty. Despite her cleverness and sharpness of mind, Jane was 'far from deeming herself to be the intellectual superior of those around her'[27] and she always regarded her sister as a far better person than herself.

9

THE LATER WRITING PERIOD
1811–1812

In February 1811 Jane started to plan *Mansfield Park*, her fourth novel. At the same time she extensively revised, or 'lop't and crop't', as she described it, the manuscript of *First Impressions* to turn it into the novel *Pride and Prejudice*. Jane continued to write in the drawing room at Chawton Cottage amidst all the daily activity of the household. Her nephew wondered how his aunt managed to concentrate in such conditions, especially when her young nephews and nieces were in the house. 'I have no doubt that I, and my sisters and cousins, in our visits to Chawton, frequently disturbed this mystic process, without having any idea of the mischief that we were doing; certainly we never should have guessed it by any signs of impatience or irritability in the writer.'[1]

Jane went to London in March 1811 to stay with Henry and Eliza. In between socialising and sight-seeing, she found time to correct the proofs of *Sense and Sensibility*, which were sent to the printers in April. In a letter to her sister, who was staying at Godmersham, Jane wrote, 'No, indeed, I am never too busy to think of *S&S*. I can no more forget it than a mother can forget her sucking child; & I am much obliged to you for your enquiries. I have had two sheets to correct, but the last only brings us to W.s first appearance.'[2]

Edward Austen's adoptive mother Mrs Knight, who was one of

the few people who knew about Jane's secret life as a writer, was looking forward to reading the soon to be published novel. Jane told Cassandra, 'I have scarcely a hope of its being out in June. – Henry does not neglect it; he has hurried the Printer, & says he will see him again to-day … I am very much gratified by Mrs K.s interest in it; & whatever may be the event of it as to my credit with her, sincerely wish her curiosity could be satisfied sooner than is now probable.'[3] Henry acted as his sister's literary agent and conducted all negotiations with her publisher.

During her stay in London Jane met her godfather Samuel Cooke and his family. She went with her cousin Mary Cooke to the Liverpool Museum in Piccadilly to see the natural history exhibits, and then to the gallery of the British Institution in Pall Mall. In a letter to Cassandra Jane wrote, 'I had some amusement at each, tho' my preference for Men & Women always inclines me to attend more to the company than the sight.'[4]

Jane described how, on another day, she walked into London from Henry's house in Sloane Street, which was at that time a rural suburb of the capital. She wrote,

Wednesday was likewise a day of great doings, for Manon (Henry's servant) & I took our walk to Grafton House, & I have a good deal to say on that subject. I am sorry to tell you that I am getting very extravagant & spending all my Money; & what is worse for *you*, I have been spending yours too; for in a Linendraper's shop to which I went for Checkd Muslin, & for which I was obliged to give seven shillings a yard, I was tempted by a pretty coloured muslin, & bought 10 yds of it, on the chance of your liking it; – but at the same time if it shd not suit you, you must not think yourself at all obliged to take it; it is only 3/6 pr yd, & I shd not in the least mind keeping the whole. – In texture, it is just what we prefer, but in its resemblance to green cruels I must own it is not great, for the pattern is a small red spot.[5]

Jane enjoyed this shopping expedition, and told Cassandra that she was 'very well satisfied' with her purchases.

On this visit to London Jane met a number of Henry's and Eliza's friends, including a family of French émigrés. She described all the 'little parties' she was taken to as 'very pleasant'. The highlight of this visit was a party hosted by Eliza where Jane met several people she was already acquainted with. She described this party in detail to her sister.

> Our party went off extremely well. There were many solicitudes, alarms & vexations beforehand of course, but at last everything was quite right. The rooms were dressed up with flowers &C, & looked very pretty … At half past 7 arrived the Musicians in two Hackney coaches, & by 8 the lordly Company began to appear. Among the earliest were George & Mary Cooke, & I spent the greatest part of the eveng very pleasantly with them. – The Drawg room being soon hotter than we liked, we placed ourselves in the connecting Passage, which was comparatively cool, & gave us all the advantage of the Music at a pleasant distance, as well as that of the first veiw (*sic*) of every new comer. – I was quite surrounded by acquaintance, especially gentlemen.[6]

After returning home in May, Jane wrote a series of letters to Cassandra that reveal how much she was enjoying life at Chawton Cottage. The beautiful garden, full of flowers and fruit, was a particular pleasure to her, as the following description shows: 'You cannot imagine, it is not in Human Nature to imagine what a nice walk we have round the Orchard. The row of Beech look very well indeed, & so does the young Quickset hedge in the Garden. – I hear to-day that an Apricot has been detected on one of the Trees. Yesterday I had the agreeable surprise of finding several scarlet strawberries quite ripe; – had *You* been at home, this would have been a pleasure lost. There are more Gooseberries & fewer Currants than I thought at first. – We must buy currants for our wine.'[7]

Jane reported news of their neighbours, and reminded Cassandra to collect pieces of fabric for a patchwork quilt they were making with their mother. This picture of domestic bliss was marred only by references to Mrs Austen's poor health and a comment on the Battle of Almeida, which was in the news at that time. Jane rarely referred to events of the day in her letters and never expressed an opinion on political matters.

Later that summer Charles Austen returned to England with his family. Jane's delight at seeing her brother again can be imagined from reading Cassandra's account of his return in a letter to her cousin Phylly Walter: 'After an absence from England of almost seven years you may guess the pleasure which having him amongst us again occasion'd. He is grown a little older in all that time, but we had the pleasure of seeing him return in good health and unchanged in mind. His Bermudan wife is a very pleasing little woman, she is gentle & amiable in her manners & appears to make him very happy. They have two pretty little girls.'[8]

Charles's next posting as commander of HMS *Namur*, a guard ship anchored off the Kent coast, kept him much closer to his family.

As the year progressed Jane eagerly awaited the publication of *Sense and Sensibility*. Only a few people were aware of this imminent event, namely Mrs Austen, Cassandra, Martha Lloyd, Jane's brothers and their wives, the Leigh-Perrotts, Mrs Knight and Jane's niece, Fanny. The secret was not even revealed to Anna, Edward or Caroline Austen. *Sense and Sensibility* was finally published at the end of October 1811. Its publication was announced in two London newspapers, *The Star* and *The Morning Chronicle*. The novel, which was published in three volumes, priced at 15 shillings, began to sell immediately and continued to sell steadily. The sales were helped by two favourable reviews. Several prominent people are known to have read the novel soon after it was published, including members of the royal family, the Countess of Bessborough and the Spencer family at Althorp House. On 22 January 1812 Princess Charlotte recorded her opinion of the novel: 'Sence and Sencibility (*sic*) I have just finished reading; it certainly is interesting, & you feel quite one of the company … I must say it interested me much.'[9]

Jane's reaction to the publication of her first novel is not known, but her achievement made up for past disappointments and encouraged her to press on with the revision of *First Impressions*. In their biography, William and Richard Austen-Leigh commented on the importance of the favourable reception of *Sense and Sensibility*. 'Had it been a failure, and an expense to its author, she would hardly have dared, nor could she have afforded, to make a second venture. On the success of *Sense and Sensibility*, we may say, depended the existence of *Pride and Prejudice*. Now she could return with renewed spirit to the preparation of the more famous work which was to follow, and on which she had already been engaged for some time, concurrently with her first-published novel.'[10]

The Austen-Leighs also commented on how, at this time, Jane was living in two worlds, the real world and her own imaginary one: 'But besides all these living objects of interest, Jane also had her own separate and peculiar world peopled by the creations of her own bright imagination which by degrees became more and more real to her as she found others accepting and admiring them.'[11]

The year 1812 was a busy one for visiting and receiving visitors at Chawton. Jane enjoyed the company of Edward and Fanny for several weeks, and she and her mother went to stay at Steventon Rectory. This was the last time Mrs Austen stayed away from Chawton Cottage, as related by William and Richard Austen-Leigh: 'In June, Jane went with her mother to stay for a fortnight at Steventon Rectory, the last visit ever paid by Mrs Austen to any place. When she determined never to leave home again, she said that her latest visit should be to her eldest son. Accordingly she went, and took a final farewell of the place where nearly the whole of her married life was spent. She was then seventy two years old, and lived on for sixteen more, but she kept her resolution and never again left Chawton Cottage for a single night.'[12]

When Jane and her mother left Steventon they brought Anna home with them for a three-month stay. It was during this time that Anna's relationship with Jane deepened, as she recalled in her memoir. 'The two years before my marriage, & the two or three years after, when we lived, as you know almost close to Chawton when the original 17 years between us seemed to shrink to 7.'[13]

Anna remembered how they enjoyed laughing at novels together.

> It was my great amusement during one summer visit at Chawton to procure Novels from the circulating Library at Alton, & after running them over to relate the stories to Aunt Jane. I may say it was her amusement also, as she sat busily stitching away at a work of charity, in which I fear that I took myself no more useful part. Greatly we both enjoyed it, one piece of absurdity leading to another, till Aunt Cassandra fatigued with her own share of laughter wd. exclaim 'How can you both be so foolish?' – & beg us to leave off.[14]

During this visit a comical incident occurred, when Anna went to the library with both of her aunts. She picked up a copy of *Sense and Sensibility*, and having no idea who the author was, threw it onto the counter and declared contemptuously, 'Oh that must be rubbish I am sure from the title.' Her aunts were greatly amused but did not divulge their secret.[15]

In October 1812 Mrs Knight died in Canterbury. Edward and his children officially took the name of Knight, which was a condition of his inheritance of the Knight estates. Mrs Knight had been fond of Jane and had helped her with gifts of money, as well as taking an interest in her writing.

Around this time Jane sold the copyright of the revised novel *First*

Impressions, which had been renamed *Pride and Prejudice*. This title change was necessary because it was discovered that the title *First Impressions* had already been used by another author. The idea for the new title came from Fanny Burney's novel *Cecilia*, in which the phrase 'pride and prejudice' appeared. Jane described the sale of her manuscript in a letter written to Martha Lloyd in November. '*P.&P.* is sold. – Egerton gives £110 for it. – I would rather have had £150, but we could not both be pleased, & I am not at all surprised that he should not chuse (*sic*) to hazard so much – Its being sold will I hope be a great saving of Trouble to Henry, & therefore must be welcome to me. – The Money is to be paid at the end of the twelvemonth.'[16]

Pride and Prejudice was published in January 1813. Meanwhile *Sense and Sensibility* continued to sell well, and eventually made a considerable profit. Henry Austen described Jane's reaction to the money she earned from her first novel, and its favourable reception.

> She could scarcely believe what she termed her great good fortune, when *Sense and Sensibility* produced a clear profit of about £150. Few so gifted were so truly unpretending. She regarded the above sum as a prodigious recompense for that which had cost her nothing. Her readers, perhaps, will wonder that such a work produced so little, at a time when some authors have received more guineas than they have written lines. But the public has not been unjust; and our authoress was far from thinking it so. Most gratifying to her was the applause which from time to time reached her ears from those who were competent to discriminate.[17]

Jane may have valued the praise she received for *Sense and Sensibility* more than the money she made from it, but £150 was a large sum to her and it considerably improved her financial position.

10

THE LATER WRITING PERIOD
1813–1814

The first advertisement for *Pride and Prejudice* appeared in *The Morning Chronicle* on 28 January 1813. Jane's anonymity as the author was maintained with the description 'by the Author of *Sense and Sensibility*' on the title page. The novel, which was in three volumes, was priced at eighteen shillings. On 29 January an excited Jane wrote to inform Cassandra, who was on another visit to Kent, that she had received her copy. 'I want to tell you that I have got my own darling Child from London; – on Wednesday I received one copy, sent down by Falknor, with three lines from Henry to say that he had given another to Charles & sent a 3*d* by the Coach to Godmersham; just the two Sets which I was least eager for the disposal of. I wrote to him immediately to beg for my other two Sets.'[1]

Jane went on to describe how she read some of the first volume to a neighbour, without her suspecting that Jane was the author.

Miss Benn dined with us the very day of the Books coming, & in the eveng we set fairly at it & read half the 1st vol. to her – prefacing that having intelligence from Henry that such a work wd soon appear we had desired him to send it whenever it came out – & I believe it passed with her unsuspected. – She was amused, poor soul! *that* she cd not help, you know, with two such people to lead the way; but she really does seem to admire Elizabeth. I must confess that *I* think her as delightful a creature as ever appeared in print, & how I shall be able to tolerate those who do not like *her* at least, I do not know.[2]

Jane's description of *Pride and Prejudice* as her 'own darling child' is an interesting one. She had previously written that she could 'no more forget' *Sense and Sensibility* than a mother could forget 'a sucking child'. It appears that Jane had come to regard her books as substitute children. Jane was only too aware that if she had become a wife and mother, as was expected of women in Georgian England, it would probably have ended her writing career. The demands of marriage, constant childbearing and motherhood would not have been compatible with writing.

According to William and Richard Austen-Leigh the publication of *Pride and Prejudice* was 'the central point' in Jane's life and 'she appeared, indeed, to be rather of that opinion herself, so far as her modest, unassuming nature would allow her to attribute importance to one of her own works'.[3]

Pride and Prejudice, like Jane's first novel, was well received by the literary world. The first review, which appeared in *The British Critic* in February 1813, described it in glowing terms: 'It is very far superior to almost all the publications of the kind which have lately come before us. It has a very unexceptionable tendency, the story is well told, the characters remarkably well drawn and supported, and written with great spirit as well as vigour … we have perused these volumes with much satisfaction and amusement, and entertain very little doubt that their successful circulation will induce the author to similar exertions.'[4]

The author of an equally positive article in *The Critical Review* in March 1813 considered that *Pride and Prejudice* 'rises very superior to any novel we have lately met with in the delineation of domestic scenes. Nor is there one character which appears flat, or obtrudes itself upon the notice of the reader with troublesome impertinence. There is not one person in the drama with whom we could readily dispense;– they have all their proper places; and fill their several stations, with great credit to themselves, and much satisfaction to the reader.'[5]

The novel soon became very popular with the reading public and some well-known people expressed their favourable opinion of it. These included the dramatist Richard Sheridan, who declared it to be 'one of the cleverest things' he had ever read, and Miss Millbanke, the future Lady Byron, who described it as 'the most probable fiction I have ever read'.[6] Many readers tried, but failed, to guess the identity of the novel's lady author. One prominent literary gentleman, reflecting the prevalent notions about female intelligence, said, 'I should like to know who is the author, for it is much too clever to have been written by a woman.'[7] As with *Sense and Sensibility*, Jane was most concerned with the reaction of her family and friends to her second-published novel. Jane wrote to Cassandra saying, 'I am exceedingly pleased that you can say what you do, after having gone thro' the whole work – & Fanny's praise is very gratifying. My hopes were tolerably strong of her, but nothing like a certainty.'[8]

Jane was delighted to hear from Henry, who was on holiday in Scotland, that the novel was admired there, and also from her friend Miss Sharp that it was popular in Ireland.

Amidst all the excitement of *Pride and Prejudice* being published, life at Chawton Cottage carried on much as usual. Jane continued to read, sew, go for long walks, and pay and receive visits. A frequent visitor to the cottage was Charlotte-Maria Middleton, a young lady whose family were at one time the tenants of Chawton Great House. Charlotte-Maria later recorded the following memory of Jane: 'I remember her as a tall thin *spare* person, with very high cheekbones great colour – sparkling Eyes not large but joyous and intelligent – her keen sense of humour I quite remember ... We saw her often She was a most kind & enjoyable person *to Children* but somewhat stiff & cold to strangers. She used to sit at Table at Dinner parties without uttering much probably collecting matter for her charming novels which in those days we knew nothing about ... my remembrance of Jane is that of her entering into all Childrens Games & liking her extremely.'[9]

In April 1813 Jane travelled to London to help nurse her sister-in-law Eliza, who had been very ill for some time. Jane had always enjoyed a close relationship with Eliza, and her death a few days later caused Jane much grief. This tragic event was described by William and Richard Austen-Leigh. 'On 25th April 1813, occurred the death of Eliza, Henry Austen's wife. She had suffered from a long and painful illness, and the end was a release at last. These circumstances would diminish the grief felt at her loss; but the event must have carried their minds back to early days at Steventon; and Jane was sure to remember with gratitude the affection and attention which Eliza had bestowed upon her much younger cousin.'[10]

Jane helped Henry to wind up his wife's affairs. After Eliza's death Henry moved from Sloane Street to chambers over his bank at 10 Henrietta Street, Covent Garden. Due to their state of mourning there were no trips to the theatre while Jane was in London, but Henry did take his sister to three picture galleries. Jane, whose mind was full of her fictional characters, spotted a portrait of a lady who looked just like Jane Bingley in *Pride and Prejudice*. She described this discovery in a letter to Cassandra, at home in Chawton.

To my great amusement, Henry & I went to the Exhibition in Spring Gardens. It is not thought a good collection, but I was very well pleased – particularly (pray tell Fanny) with a small portrait of Mrs

Bingley, excessively like her. I went in hopes of seeing one of her Sister, but there was no Mrs Darcy; – perhaps however, I may find her in the Great Exhibition which we shall go to, if we have time; – I have no chance of her in the collection of Sir Joshua Reynolds's Paintings which is now shewing in Pall Mall, & which we are also to visit. – Mrs Bingley's is exactly herself, size, shaped face, features & sweetness; there never was a greater likeness. She is dressed in a white gown, with green ornaments, which convinces me of what I had always supposed, that green was a favourite colour with her. I dare say Mrs D. will be in yellow.[11]

Jane later added, 'We have been both to the Exhibition & Sir J. Reynolds,– and I am disappointed, for there was nothing like Mrs D. at either – I can only imagine that Mr D. prizes any Picture of her too much to like it should be exposed to the public eye – I can imagine he wd have that sort (of) feeling – that mixture of Love, Pride and Delicacy.'[12]

After her return home Jane was in almost daily contact with Edward and his children at Chawton Great House. The relationship between Jane and her niece Fanny grew closer over the summer months of 1813, with Fanny recording in her diary that they spent 'delicious' times together. Jane told her brother Frank, in a letter, how much she saw of Edward and his family. 'We go on in the most comfortable way, very frequently dining together, & always meeting in some part of every day.'[13]

Jane also informed Frank about the sales of *Sense and Sensibility* and the progress of her third novel, which was nearing completion. 'You will be glad to hear that every Copy of *S. & S.* is sold & that it has brought me £140 – besides the Copyright, if that shd ever be of any value. – I have now therefore written myself into £250 – which only makes me long for more. – I have something in hand – which I hope on the credit of *P. & P.* will sell well, tho' not half so entertaining.'[14]

In August Anna Austen announced her engagement to Ben

Lefroy, the son of Jane's late dear friend Anne Lefroy. Jane was concerned at this news because of the difference in their characters, and the fact that Ben had no settled occupation. Rather worryingly, Ben had turned down a curacy because he had not made up his mind to take orders at such a young age. He said that he would rather give Anna up than be pushed into doing something he was not ready for.

By September 1813 Jane had ceased all attempts to conceal that she was the author of two popular novels. She informed her brother Frank that 'the Secret has spread so far as to be scarcely the Shadow of a secret now … Henry heard *P. & P.* warmly praised in Scotland, by Lady Robt Kerr & another Lady; – & what does he do in the warmth of his Brotherly vanity & Love, but immediately tell them who wrote it! – A Thing once set going in that way – one knows how it spreads! – and he, dear Creature, has set it going so much more than once. I know it is all done from affection & partiality…'[15]

Jane told Frank that when *Mansfield Park* was published she would 'not even attempt to tell Lies about it. – I shall rather try to make all the Money than all the Mystery I can of it. – People shall pay for their Knowledge if I can make them.'[16]

Edward and Anna Austen were also aware by this time of their aunt's secret life as a published author. Edward, who had read both novels, wrote a poem to his aunt in recognition of her achievement which began with the lines

No words can express, my dear Aunt, my surprise
Or make you conceive how I opened my eyes,
Like a pig Butcher Pile has just struck with his knife,
When I heard for the very first time in my life
That I had the honour to have a relation
Whose works were dispersed through the whole of the nation…[17]

When her brother Edward and his family returned to Godmersham in September, Jane went with them. This was her first visit to Kent in four years and was to be her last. While most of Edward's family travelled in convoy back to Kent, he took Jane and his three eldest daughters home via London. During her three days in the capital Jane spent some of the money she had earned from *Sense and Sensibility*. She bought some dress fabric for Cassandra which, she wrote to inform her, was 'a present. Do not refuse me. I am very rich.'[18] This must have been a liberating experience for Jane, after years of struggling on an inadequate allowance.

Jane's last visit to Godmersham was as busy as all the previous ones. She wrote to Cassandra that 'in this House there is a constant succession of small events, somebody is always going or coming'.[19]

Jane joined once more in the hectic social life of the Kent upper classes. She found some of the company she met less than inspiring, however, as this extract from a letter to her sister shows: 'Our visit to the Tyldens is over. My Brother, Fanny, Edwd & I went; … There was nothing entertaining, or out of the common way. We met only Tyldens and double Tyldens. A Whist Table for the Gentlemen, a grown-up musical young Lady to play Backgammon with Fanny, & engravings of the Colleges at Cambridge for me…'[20]

Of some visitors to Godmersham Jane wrote, 'Lady Eliz. Hatton & Annamaria called here this morng, – Yes, they called, – but I do not think I can say anything more about them. They came & they sat & they went.'[21] The social events which Jane did enjoy included a ball, which she attended as Fanny's chaperone. Jane was now too old to dance at balls herself, but, as she explained to her sister, 'I find many douceurs in being a sort of Chaperon for I am put on the Sofa near the Fire & can drink as much wine as I like.'[22]

Despite the constant bustle of life at Godmersham, Jane found an opportunity to write whenever she stayed there. Her niece Marianne remembered how her aunt always took her current manuscript to work on.

I remember that when Aunt Jane came to us at Godmersham she used to bring the manuscript of whatever novel she was writing with her, and would shut herself up with my elder sisters in one of the bedrooms to read them aloud. I and the younger ones used to hear peals of laughter through the door, and thought it very hard that we should be shut out from what was so delightful. I also remember how Aunt Jane would sit quietly working beside the fire in the library, saying nothing for a good while, and then would suddenly burst out laughing, jump up and run across the room to a table where pens and paper were lying, write something down, and then come back to the fire and go on quietly working as before.[23]

Louisa Knight remembered that her aunt was '…very absent indeed. She would sit silent awhile, then rub her hands, laugh to herself and run up to her room.'[24] Louisa also recalled going to her aunt's bedroom one evening during this visit. Jane's niece retained a vivid image of her aunt as she prepared for dinner. 'She had large dark eyes and a brilliant complexion, and long, long black hair down to her knees.'[25]

In October, while Jane was at Godmersham, second editions of both *Sense and Sensibility* and *Pride and Prejudice* were brought out. It is thought that *Mansfield Park* was accepted for publication by Thomas Egerton a few weeks later. Egerton clearly did not expect Jane's third novel to be as successful as the previous one, and agreed to publish on a commission-only basis.

At the end of her stay in Kent, Jane went to London to see Henry. While she was there an attempt was made to introduce her to a literary circle, as described by Henry in his *Memoir*.

Miss Austen was on a visit in London soon after the publication of Mansfield Park; a nobleman, personally unknown to her, but who had good reasons for considering her to be the authoress of that work, was desirous of her joining a literary circle at his house. He communicated his wish in the politest manner through a mutual friend, adding, what his Lordship doubtless thought would be an irresistible inducement, that the celebrated Madame de Stael would be of the party. Miss Austen immediately declined the invitation. To her truly delicate mind such a display would have given pain instead of pleasure.[26]

In January 1814 Jane began to write *Emma*, telling her family that this novel would have 'a heroine whom no-one but myself would much like'. William and Richard Austen-Leigh wrote in their biography, 'All through this year and the early part of the next *Emma* was assiduously worked at. Although polished to the highest degree, it was more quickly composed than any previous work and gave evidence of a practised hand.'[27]

Jane probably also checked the proofs of *Mansfield Park* around this time. Henry Austen read a proof copy of the novel as he and Jane travelled to London on 1 March. In a letter to Cassandra describing their journey, Jane wrote, 'We did not begin reading till Bentley Green. Henry's approbation hitherto is even equal to my wishes; he says it is different from the other two, but does not appear to think it at all inferior ... & gives great praise to the drawing of the Characters.'[28]

A few days later Jane wrote, 'Henry has this moment said that he likes my *M.P* better & better; he is in the 3d vol ...'[29] and 'Henry has finished *Mansfield Park*, & his approbation has not lessened. He found the last half of the volume *extremely interesting*.'[30]

On 5 April, when Jane was back home in Chawton, hostilities between England and France ceased once more. Fanny Knight wrote in her diary, 'A most glorious week of news. Buonoparte vanquished and dethroned and the Bourbons re-established.'

Peace celebrations were held in towns across the country, including Alton. Fanny, who was staying at Chawton, recorded that she went to see the illuminations there, and it is likely that her aunt went with her. When the war ended Frank Austen returned to England and lived on shore while he awaited his next posting. He saw more of his family, especially when he was staying at Chawton Great House. Charles remained at sea, commanding the *Namur*.

On 9 May 1814, *Mansfield Park* was published. It was advertised in both *The Morning Chronicle* and *The Star*, described as being 'by the Author of *Sense and Sensibility* and *Pride and Prejudice*'. It was sold for the same price as *Pride and Prejudice* – eighteen shillings for the three volumes. Unlike Jane's first two novels, *Mansfield Park* was not reviewed in the press, but this did not prevent it from selling well. Jane wrote down the opinions of her family and friends on her new novel. Cassandra thought it 'quite as clever, tho' not so brilliant as *Pride and Prejudice*'. Frank's view was similar: 'We certainly do not think it as a *whole*, equal to *P. & P.* – but it has many & great beauties. Fanny is a delightful character! and Aunt Norris is a great favourite of mine. The Characters are natural & well supported, & many of the Dialogues excellent. – You need not fear the publication being considered as discreditable to the talents of its Author.'[31]

Jane's friend Anne Sharp, although she thought the characterisation good, also preferred *Pride and Prejudice*. Among other recorded opinions is the qualified praise of Lady Anne Romilly, who enquired of the novelist Maria Edgeworth, 'Have you read *Mansfield Park*? It has been pretty generally admired here (London) and I think all novels must be that are true to life which this is, with a good strong vein of principle running thro' the whole. It has not however that elevation of virtue, something beyond nature, that gives the greatest charm to a novel, but still it is real natural every day life, and will amuse an idle hour in spite of its faults.'[32]

Jane would have been particularly pleased with the praise for her 'natural' characters and the novel's realism, as these were effects which she particularly sought to achieve.

In the summer of 1814 Jane took a break from writing to spend two weeks with her godfather, the Reverend Samuel Cooke, and his family in Great Bookham in Surrey. The Cookes were reading *Mansfield Park* during her visit and Jane informed Cassandra that 'they admire *Mansfield Park* exceedingly. Mr Cooke says it is the most sensible novel he ever read and the manner in which I treat the clergy delights them very much.'[33]

Emma was very much on Jane's mind while she was in Surrey because it was set in that county. There have been a number of attempts to identify the locality of the fictional town Highbury, where most of the action in the novel takes place. It has been variously identified with Leatherhead, Dorking and Esher. William and Richard Austen-Leigh discussed this in their biography and concluded that, although Jane used her visit to 'the neighbourhood of Leatherhead and Box Hill to verify geographical and other details for her new work', it was most likely that she 'purposely avoided identifying it with any one village, while sufficiently defining its position in the county of Surrey'.[34] As Jane used qualities and characteristics from a variety of real people when creating her fictional characters, it is likely that she took features from a number of real places when creating her fictional localities. Jane herself once said that 'it was her desire to create not to reproduce'.[35]

While Jane was busy writing *Emma* she found the time to help and encourage her niece Anna, who was attempting to write a novel of her own. Anna sent each chapter to Jane for criticism and advice. In a letter to her niece written in July 1814, Jane wrote, 'I am very much obliged to you for sending your MS. It has entertained me extremely, all of us indeed; I read it aloud to your G.M. – & At C. – and we were all very much pleased ... A few verbal corrections were all that I felt tempted to make.'[36]

Jane's advice to Anna provides an interesting insight into her own views on the best way to write a novel, and also reveals the high standards she imposed on herself. Jane stressed the importance of accuracy, including topographical accuracy, the drawing of natural and consistent characters, and the creation of an illusion of truth when writing fiction. She advised Anna to write only about types of people and places she was familiar with, to avoid giving 'false representations'. A paragraph in another letter described exactly what she was doing herself as she wrote *Emma*. 'You are now collecting your People delightfully, getting them exactly into such a spot as is the delight of my life; – 3 or 4 Families in a Country Village is the very thing to work on – & I hope you will write a great deal more, & make full use of them while they are so favourably arranged.'[37]

Jane's work on the manuscript of *Emma* was interrupted in September of this year by the news of the death of her brother Charles's wife Fanny, a few days after the birth of her fourth daughter, and the death of the baby soon after. The loss of another sister-in-law following childbirth must have reminded Jane of the risks she would have been exposed to if she had become a wife and mother herself. On the death of his wife, Charles resigned his command of the *Namur* in order to arrange for the care of his three daughters. After leaving them in the care of their maternal grandparents in London, Charles returned to work as commander of the *Phoenix*, which was based in the Mediterranean Sea. Further anxiety was caused to the Austen family, at this already difficult time, when a claim was made on Edward's Hampshire estate by some heirs-at-law of the Knight family. This was the beginning of a lawsuit which dragged on for a number of years, and could have resulted in the Austen ladies losing their home.

There was some happier news in November when Anna married Ben Lefroy, who had finally agreed to take holy orders. The young couple moved to the village of Hendon, on the outskirts of London.

Anna continued to send chapter after chapter of her novel to Jane, which made her aunt remark, 'I only wish other people of my acquaintance could compose so rapidly.'[38]

Towards the end of the year Jane was in correspondence with her niece Fanny, who had sought her advice on a romantic attachment. Fanny was in turmoil over her feelings for a young man called John Plumptre, whom she had been seeing for some time. Jane gave her niece some sensible advice, taking into account the feelings of both parties. In one letter she wrote, 'Your mistake has been one that thousands of women fall into. He was the *first* young Man who attached himself to you. That was the charm, & most powerful it is.'[39]

Jane begged Fanny not to consider accepting John unless she really liked him, advising that 'anything is to be preferred or endured rather than marrying without Affection'[40] and that 'nothing can be compared to the misery of being bound without Love, bound to one, and preferring another'.[41]

She was careful to add 'your own feelings & none but your own, should determine such an important point'.[42] Fanny eventually decided to discourage John Plumptre. Jane's belief in the importance of love in marriage is evident in her novels. Jane's sound sense and wisdom led Edward Austen-Leigh to comment that her nieces 'knew what a sympathising friend and judicious advisor they found her in many difficulties and doubts of early womanhood'.[43] Jane was never too busy to find time to help her two young nieces, who did not have a mother to turn to for advice.

By November 1814 the first edition of *Mansfield Park* was all sold out, and Jane had made a handsome profit of £350. The possibility of a second edition was discussed with Thomas Egerton but, for some unknown reason, his company did not go ahead. This may be why the manuscript of *Emma*, which was nearing completion, was sent to another publisher.

53. Steventon Rectory, where Jane spent the first twenty-five years of her life.

54. Steventon Manor House, which belonged to the Knight family and was part of the estates inherited by Edward Austen.

Top of page: 55. Silhouettes of Rev. George Austen (Jane's father), Mrs Cassandra Austen (Jane's mother) and Cassandra Austen (Jane's sister).
Above left: 56. Jane, painted by Cassandra Austen.
Above right: 57. James Austen, Jane's eldest brother.
Left: 58. James-Edward Austen-Leigh, Jane's nephew and the author of the first biography of her.

Above: 59. The Reverend Austen presenting his son Edward to Mr and Mrs Thomas Knight. A silhouette by the London artist William Wellings.
Right: 60. Edward Austen, a portrait painted while he was on a Grand Tour of Europe.
Below: 61. Godmersham House and Park, Kent as they appeared towards the end of the eighteenth century. The grand Palladian style house was built by Thomas Knight I, a cousin of Jane's father. The Knight estates were inherited by Jane's brother Edward in 1797.

Left & above: 62 & 63. The Hall, Godmersham House.
Below: 64. The kitchen of an eighteenth-century country inn. Jane stopped in country inns such as this on her long journeys to Kent.

Above left: 65. Thomas Knight, Edward Austen's adoptive father, painted by George Romney.
Above right: 66. Catherine Knight, Edward Austen's adoptive mother, painted by George Romney.

67. The Circus, Bath. The Circus, designed by John Wood the Elder, was adjacent to Gay Street where Jane lived briefly in 1805.

68. The Assembly Rooms, which Jane visited frequently when she lived in Bath.

Above: 69. The Old Assembly Rooms or Lower Rooms, Bath. Jane frequented these assembly rooms which were situated on Terrace Walk near South Parade. This fine building, which was built in 1708, was burnt to the ground in 1820.

Left: 70. A corner of the drawing room of 4 Sydney Place.

Below: 71. Sydney Gardens, Bath, 1804. Jane's home at 4 Sydney Place overlooked the gardens.

72. The interior of the Pump Room, Bath, 1804. Jane visited the Pump Room with her uncle when he took the waters.

73. The Pump Room and Queen's Bath, 1804.

74. Milsom Street, Bath. Jane's aunt was accused of stealing a piece of lace from a shop in this exclusive street.

Above left: 75. Interior of the Pump Room.
Above centre: 76. Trim Bridge, Bath. Jane moved to nearby Trim Street in 1806.
Above right: 77. A sedan chair, a popular form of transport in Georgian towns and cities.

Left: 78. *The Original Bath Mail Coach*, a familiar sight on the roads around Bath when Jane lived there.
Below: 79. The house in Lyme Regis where Jane stayed on holiday with her parents in 1804.

80. *On the Sands at Worthing, 1808*. Jane went on holiday to Worthing in 1805.

81. *An Airing in Hyde Park, 1793*. Jane enjoyed taking carriage rides in the parks of London.

82. Entrance to Hyde Park, 1756. In April 1811 Jane and her sister-in-law had to get out of their carriage near here because their horses refused to go any further.

Above: 83. Pall Mall, London. Jane visited an exhibition of Joshua Reynolds' paintings here in 1811.
Right: 84. The Theatre Royal, Drury Lane was another entertainment venue which Jane liked to visit.

85. Shop Interior, Old Bond Street, 1817. Jane enjoyed shopping in London's West End.

Above: 86. Carlton House, Pall Mall, the home of the prince regent. Jane visited Carlton House in 1816 at the invitation of the prince.
Right: 87. The Great Staircase at Carlton House.

Left: 88. A corner of the Golden Drawing Room, Carlton House. Jane was shown around the house on her visit in 1816.
Above: 89. The prince regent, a keen reader of Jane's novels. At the request of his librarian Jane dedicated *Emma* to the prince.

SENSE
AND
SENSIBILITY:

A NOVEL.

IN THREE VOLUMES.

BY A LADY.

VOL. I.

London:
PRINTED FOR THE AUTHOR,
By C. Roworth, Bell-yard, Temple-bar,
AND PUBLISHED BY T. EGERTON, WHITEHALL.
1811.

Above: 90. The title page of the first edition of *Sense and Sensibility*.
Above right: 91. Frontispiece to the 1833 edition of *Sense and Sensibility*.
Right: 92. Frontispiece to the 1833 edition of *Pride and Prejudice*.

Above left: 93. Frontispiece
to the 1833 edition of
Mansfield Park.
Above: 94. Frontispiece to
the 1833 edition of *Emma*.
Left: 95. Frontispiece to the
1833 edition of *Northanger
Abbey* and *Persuasion*.

Above: 96. St Nicholas church, Chawton, where
Henry Austen was curate from 1816 to 1820.
Right: 97. Chawton Cottage, Jane's last home.
Below right: 98. Frontispiece to the second edition
of Edward Austen-Leigh's *Memoir* of Jane.
Below: 99. Pittville Pump Room, Cheltenham. Jane
went to this spa town in May 1816, a few months
after the onset of her illness.

11

THE LATER WRITING PERIOD
1815–1816

Jane took a break from writing *Emma* from Boxing Day 1814 until the middle of the following month. She and Cassandra went to stay with their friends Alethea Bigg and her sister Elizabeth Heathcote, who were living in Winchester. This was followed by two weeks in Steventon and Ashe, where they visited a number of old friends and neighbours. On her return home Jane resumed work on *Emma*, which she completed on 29 March 1815.

As Jane was writing the final pages of her novel, Napoleon escaped from his prison on the island of Elba and the war with France flared up once more. Charles Austen was involved in chasing the ships of the French and their allies in the Mediterranean. The Battle of Waterloo, which took place on 18 June, finally brought the hostilities to an end and Napoleon was sent in exile to St Helena.

James Austen's wife Mary and their daughter Caroline stayed at Chawton Cottage for several weeks during the summer of 1815. Many of the memories of her aunt, which Caroline later recorded, date from this visit. The following extracts from her memoir provide further evidence that Jane was a much-loved aunt, and a delightful companion to her nephews and nieces.

Of the two, Aunt Jane was by far my favourite – I did not *dislike* Aunt Cassandra – but if my visit had at any time chanced to fall out during *her* absence, I don't think I should have missed her – whereas, *not* to have Aunt Jane at Chawton *would* have been a blank indeed.[1]

As I grew older, I met with young companions at my Grandmother's – Of Capt. Charles Austen's motherless girls, one the eldest, Cassy – lived there chiefly, for a time – under the especial tutorage of Aunt Cassandra; and then Chawton House was for a while inhabited by Capt. Frank Austen; and he had many children – I believe we were all of us, according to our different ages and natures, very fond of our Aunt Jane.[2]

When staying at Chawton, if my two cousins, Mary Jane and Cassy were there, we often had amusements in which my Aunt was very helpful – *She* was the one to whom we always looked for help – She would furnish us with what we wanted from her wardrobe, and *she* would often be the entertaining visitor in our make beleive (*sic*) house – She amused us in various ways – once I remember in giving a conversation as between myself and my two cousins, supposed to be grown up, the day after a Ball.[3]

As I grew older, she would talk to me more seriously of my reading, and of my amusements – I had taken early to writing verses and stories, and I am sorry to think *how* I troubled her with reading them. She was very kind about it, and always had some praise to bestow but at last she warned me against spending too much time upon them – She said – how well I recollect it! that she *knew* writing stories was a great amusement, and *she* thought a harmless one – tho' many people, she was aware, thought otherwise – but that at my age it would be bad for me to be much taken up with my own compositions…[4]

In August Jane began to write her sixth novel, *Persuasion*. Around the same time the manuscript of *Emma* was sent to the well-known publisher John Murray of Albemarle Street in London. His reader was very impressed with the novel and reported that he had 'nothing but good to say' of it. It may have been negotiations with her publishers that took Jane to London in early October. In a letter dated 17 to 18 of that month, Jane informed her sister that 'Mr Murray's Letter is come; he is a Rogue of course, but a civil one. He offers £450 – but wants to have the Copyright of *M.P.* and *S. & S.* included. It will end in my publishing for myself I dare say. – He sends more praise however than I expected. It is an amusing Letter. You shall see it.'[5]

There was a delay in Jane's response to John Murray's letter regarding *Emma* because her brother Henry became very ill. It started with what Jane described as 'a bilious attack with fever', which soon turned into something more serious. He was initially attended by a Mr Haden, an apothecary from Sloane Street, who attempted to cure the fever by blood-letting. Henry soon became so dangerously ill that James, Edward and Cassandra were summoned to his bedside. At some stage one of the prince regent's physicians was called in to treat him. After a week of anxiety, however, Henry began to recover and his brothers were able to return home. Jane and Cassandra remained in London to nurse Henry back to full health.

Jane checked the proof sheets of *Emma* while she watched over her brother. In early November Henry was well enough to dictate the following letter to John Murray.

Severe Illness has confined me to my Bed ever since I received Yours of ye 15th – I cannot yet hold a pen, & employ an Amanuensis. – The Politeness & Perspicuity of your Letter equally claim my earliest Exertion. – Your official opinion of the Merits of *Emma*, is very valuable & satisfactory. – Though I venture to differ occasionally from your Critique, yet I assure you the Quantum of your commendation rather exceeds than falls short of the

Author's expectation and my own. – The Terms you offer are so very inferior to what we had expected, that I am apprehensive of having made some great Error in my Arithmetical Calculation. – On the subject of the expence (*sic*) & profit of publishing, you must be much better informed than I am; – but Documents in my possession appear to prove that the Sum offered by you for the Copyright of *Sense & Sensibility, Mansfield Park, & Emma*, is not equal to the Money which my Sister has actually cleared by one very moderate Edition of *Mansfield Park* – (You Yourself expressed astonishment that so small an Edit: of such a work should have been sent into the World) – & a still smaller one of *Sense and Sensibility*.[6]

Henry's letter was to no avail, however, as Murray refused to improve his offer for the copyrights. He did, however, agree to publish 2,000 copies of *Emma*, on a commission-only basis, and to bring out a second edition of *Mansfield Park*, with a print run of 750 copies, on the same terms.

Henry's illness led to what Edward Austen-Leigh described in his *Memoir* as 'the only mark of distinction ever bestowed' on his aunt. Edward wrote,

It happened thus. In the autumn of 1815 she nursed her brother Henry through a dangerous fever and slow convalescence at his house in Hans Place. He was attended by one of the Prince Regent's physicians. All attempts to keep her name secret had at this time ceased, and though it had never appeared on a title-page, all who cared to know might easily learn it; and the friendly physician was aware that his patient's nurse was the author of *Pride and Prejudice*. Accordingly he informed her one day that the Prince was a great admirer of her novels; that he read them often, and kept a set in every one of his residences; that he himself therefore had thought it right to inform his Royal Highness that

Miss Austen was staying in London, and that the Prince had desired Mr Clarke, the librarian of Carlton House, to wait upon her. The next day Mr Clarke made his appearance, and invited her to Carlton House, saying that he had the Prince's instructions to show her the library, and other apartments, and to pay her every possible attention. The invitation was of course accepted, and during the visit to Carlton House Mr Clarke declared himself commissioned to say that if Miss Austen had any other novel forthcoming she was at liberty to dedicate it to the Prince.[7]

Jane was not, at first, inclined to dedicate any novel to the prince regent until she was advised, probably by Henry and Cassandra, to regard the invitation as a command. Jane, therefore, asked her publisher to dedicate *Emma* to the prince and later used this dedication to urge the printers, who were delaying the publication, 'to greater Dispatch and Punctuality'.[8] It was not long before Jane was able to inform Cassandra that the printer's boys were hurrying to and from Hans Place with the proof sheets of her novel.

Jane's visit to Carlton House led to an exchange of letters between her and the prince regent's librarian, the Reverend James Stanier Clarke, which must have given Jane much cause for amusement. The correspondence began when Mr Clarke, who was also the prince's chaplain, asked Jane

to delineate in some future work the Habits of Life and Character and enthusiasm of a Clergyman – who should pass his time between the metropolis & the Country – who should be something like Beatties Minstrel

Silent when glad, affectionate tho' shy
And now his look was most demurely sad
& now he laugh'd aloud yet none knew why –
Neither Goldsmith – nor La Fontaine in his Tableau de Famille

– have in my mind quite delineated an English Clergyman, at least of the present day – Fond of, & entirely engaged in Literature – no man's Enemy but his own. Pray dear Madam think of these things.[9]

Mr Clarke, who was rather full of his own importance, clearly wanted Jane to write a novel with a hero modelled on himself. When Jane wrote to inform Mr Clarke that he would receive a copy of *Emma* for the prince regent three days before it was available to the general public, she responded to his suggestion. Jane's letter is interesting because, after thanking Mr Clarke for his 'very high praise' of her other novels, she proceeded to reveal her fears that *Emma* would not live up to her readers' expectations, and to describe what she felt were her limitations as a novelist.

My greatest anxiety at present is that this 4th work shd not disgrace what was good in the others. But on this point I will do myself the justice to declare that whatever may be my wishes for its success, I am very strongly haunted by the idea that to those Readers who have preferred *P&P.* it will appear inferior in Wit, & to those who have preferred *M.P.* very inferior in good sense. Such as it is however, I hope you will do me the favour of accepting a Copy. Mr M. will have directions for sending one. I am quite honoured by your thinking me capable of drawing such a Clergyman as you gave the sketch of in your note of Nov.16. But I assure you I am *not*. The comic part of the Character I might be equal to, but not the Good, the Enthusiastic, the Literary. Such a Man's Conservation must at times be on subjects of Science & Philosophy of which I know nothing – or at least be occasionally abundant in quotations & allusions which a Woman, who like me, knows only her own Mother-tongue, & has read very little in that, would be totally without the power of giving – A Classical Education, or at any rate, a very extensive acquaintance with

English Literature, Ancient & Modern, appears to me quite Indispensable for the person who wd do any justice to your Clergyman – And I think I may boast myself to be, with all possible Vanity, the most unlearned, & uniformed Female who ever dared to be an Authoress.[10]

This last sentence must surely have been written with tongue in cheek. Even taking into account her excessive modesty, Jane could not seriously have considered this to be a fair description of herself.

Despite Jane's rejection of his proposal, Mr Clarke persisted. His next suggestion was that she should write a novel about a clergyman 'after your own fancy', and then he proposed that she write 'a high romance – illustrative of the history of the House of Cobourg'.[11] Jane turned down these suggestions also and, in her reply, once again assessed her own ability as a novelist.

You are very, very kind in your hints as to the sort of Composition which might recommend me at present, & I am fully sensible that an Historical Romance founded on the House of Saxe Cobourg might be much more to the purpose of Profit or Popularity, than such pictures of domestic Life in Country Villages as I deal in – but I could no more write a Romance than an Epic Poem. – I could not sit seriously down to write a serious Romance under any other motive than to save my Life, & if it were indispensible (*sic*) for me to keep it up & never relax into laughing at myself or other people, I am sure I should be hung before I had finished the first Chapter – No – I must keep to my own style & go on in my own Way, And though I may never succeed again in that, I am convinced that I should totally fail in any other.[12]

Jane returned to Chawton in December, having stayed with Henry until his health was fully restored. At the end of the month

Emma was published in three volumes for one guinea. The novel was dedicated to the prince regent, as requested, but the author's identity was not revealed. Once the novel was published Jane's association with the prince ended, as Caroline Austen recorded in her *Memoir*.

> My Aunt, soon after her visit to *him*, returned home, where the little adventure was talked of for a while with some interest, and afforded some amusement – In the following Spring, Mr Henry Austen ceased to reside in London, and my Aunt was never brought so near the precincts of the Court again – nor did she ever try to recall herself to the recollection of Physician, Librarian, or Prince, and so ended this little burst of Royal Patronage.[13]

Emma, like Jane's three previous published novels, began to sell steadily. She sent out her presentation copies to family and friends and, as she did with *Mansfield Park*, collected their opinions and comments on the novel. Opinion was divided, with some readers preferring it to her previous works, and others taking the opposite view. Cassandra liked *Emma* 'better than *P. & P.* – not so well as *M.P.*' Frank Austen 'liked it extremely, observing that though there might be more Wit in *P. & P.* – and an higher Morality in *MP* – yet altogether, on account of its peculiar air of Nature throughout, he preferred it to either'.[14]

Charles received his copy of the novel in the Mediterranean and wrote to say, '*Emma* arrived in time to a moment. I am delighted with her, more so I think than even with my favourite *Pride and Prejudice*, & have read it three times in the Passage.'[15]

Once again, Jane's ability to create lifelike characters was widely praised. The characters in *Emma* were so natural that Jane was accused of copying real people. Edward Austen-Leigh refuted this accusation in the following paragraphs of his *Memoir*:

Some persons have surmised that she took her characters from individuals with whom she had been acquainted. They were so lifelike that it was assumed that they must once have lived, and have been transferred bodily, as it were, into her pages. But surely such a supposition betrays an ignorance of the high prerogative of genius to create out of its own resources imaginary characters, who shall be true to nature and consistent in themselves ...[16] She did not copy individuals, but she invested her own creations with individuality of character ... Her own relations never recognised any individual in her characters; and I can call to mind several of her acquaintance whose peculiarities were very tempting and easy to be caricatured of whom there are no traces in her pages.[17]

Jane once said that she was 'too proud of my gentlemen to admit that they were only Mr A or Colonel B'.[18] However, as her nephew pointed out, she did not 'suppose that her imaginary characters were of a higher order than are to be found in nature; for she said, when speaking of two of her great favourites, Edmund Bertram and Mr Knightley: "They are very far from being what I know English gentlemen often are."'[19]

Emma was reviewed in a number of magazines and periodicals. *The British Lady's Magazine* considered it to be inferior to both *Pride and Prejudice* and *Mansfield Park*. *The Champion*, however, praised its 'easy, unaffected and fluent style' and 'the lively sketches of comfortable home-scenes'. This reviewer described Jane as 'a woman of good sense, knowledge of the world, discriminating perception and acute observation'.[20]

John Murray, who owned the *Quarterly Review*, asked Walter Scott to write a review of *Emma*. Scott praised Jane's skill in 'copying from nature as she really exists in the common walks of life, and presenting to the reader, instead of the splendid scenes of an imaginary world, a correct and striking representation of that which is daily taking place around him'.[21]

Jane sent a copy of *Emma* to her niece Anna, who had recently moved with her husband and baby daughter to Wyards, a farmhouse near Alton. The baby, Anna-Jemima, was born in October 1815 when Jane was in London nursing Henry. As Jane had not yet seen her great-niece, she sent a note with the book saying, 'As I wish very much to see *your* Jemima, I am sure you will like to see *my Emma* & have therefore great pleasure in sending it for your perusal.'[22]

It was probably early in the year 1816 that Jane decided to buy back the manuscript of her novel *Susan* from the publishers Crosby and Co. Henry Austen visited the publisher's office and found Richard Crosby willing to sell the copyright back for the same sum he had paid for it. After the deal was finished, Henry had the great satisfaction of informing Crosby that the work which he had thought not worth publishing was by the author of the popular novel *Pride and Prejudice*. Having recovered and revised her manuscript, however, Jane did not attempt to get it published. She told her niece Fanny in a letter dated 13 March 1816 that '"Miss Catherine" (*Susan*) is put upon the shelf for the present, and I do not know that she will ever come out; but I have a something ready for publication, which may, perhaps appear about a twelvemonth hence. It is short – about the length of "Catherine".'[23]

The 'something' was *Persuasion*. The fact that Jane did not expect this novel, which she described as 'ready for publication', to be published for another year shows how much time she allowed herself for perfecting her completed manuscripts.

Early in the year 1816 Jane began to feel unwell. According to William and Richard Austen-Leigh, the stress and anxiety of nursing her brother through his dangerous illness undermined her own health. Henry described the onset of his sister's illness in his *Biographical Notice*. 'The natural constitution, the regular habits, the quiet and happy occupations of our authoress, seemed to promise a long succession of amusement to the public, and a gradual increase of reputation to herself. But the symptoms of a decay, deep and incurable, began to shew themselves in the commencement of 1816. Her decline was at first deceitfully slow...'[24]

Two troubling events occurred within the Austen family at the same time as the onset of Jane's illness, and added to her anxiety. On 21 February 1816 Charles Austen's ship, the *Phoenix*, was wrecked in a hurricane off the coast of Turkey. Fortunately no lives were lost, but Charles had to endure a court-martial before being absolved of all blame. A few weeks later Henry Austen, who had always been the least stable of Jane's brothers, was declared bankrupt. As well as ending his banking career, Henry lost his position as Receiver General of Oxfordshire, which he had held since 1813, with devastating consequences. According to William and Richard Austen-Leigh,

> the banking-house of Austen, Maunde and Tilson, had closed its doors; and on March 23 1816, Henry Austen was declared a bankrupt; the immediate cause of the collapse being the failure of an Alton bank which the London firm had backed. No personal extravagance was charged against Henry; but he had the unpleasant sensation of starting life over again, and of having caused serious loss to several of his family, especially his brother Edward and Mr Leigh-Perrot, who had gone sureties for him on his appointment as Receiver General for Oxfordshire. Jane herself was fortunate in losing no more than thirteen pounds, a portion of the profits of *Mansfield Park*.

Henry Austen possessed an extraordinary elasticity of nature which made a rebound from depression easy indeed, almost inevitable in his case. He returned at once to his original intention of taking Orders, as if the intervening military and banking career had been nothing more than an interruption of his normal course.[25]

For Jane, one positive consequence of Henry's misfortune was that he left London and spent much of his time in Chawton. William and Richard Austen-Leigh remarked that 'no division or bitterness seems to have been caused in the family by these events, remarkable proof of the strong affection which united them'.[26]

On 2 May, Edward and Fanny came to stay at Chawton. With Fanny's help, Jane used the many suggestions and pieces of advice she had received from different people to write *A Plan of a Novel According to Hints from Various Quarters*. This humorous piece of writing included the suggestions given to Jane the previous year by the prince regent's librarian. The plan concluded with a list of the contributors whose hints had been used.

On 22 May Jane travelled with Cassandra to the spa town of Cheltenham, in the hope that she would benefit from taking the waters, as described by their niece Caroline:

In May, 1816 my two Aunts went for a few weeks to Cheltenham … It was a journey in those days, to go from Hampshire into Gloucestershire and their first stage was to Steventon – They remained one whole day, and left my cousin Cassy to remain with us during their absence.

They made also a short stay at Mr Fowle's at Kintbury I believe *that* was, as they returned – Mrs Dexter, then Mary Jane Fowle, told me afterwards, that Aunt Jane went over the old places, and recalled old recollections associated with them, in a very particular manner – looked at them, my cousin thought, as if she never expected to see them again – The Kintbury family, during that visit, received an impression that her health was failing – altho' they did not know of any particular malady.[27]

Jane's nephew Edward wrote, 'I cannot tell how soon she was aware of the serious nature of her malady. By God's mercy it was not attended with much suffering ... but the progress of the disease became more and more manifest as the year advanced.'[28]

Jane's doctors were unable to diagnose her illness, and its exact nature has never been firmly established. The symptoms of weakness and back pain in the early stages, followed by skin discolouration, suggest that she may have suffered from Addison's Disease, a chronic adrenal disorder. It has, however, also been suggested that her illness was a form of lymphoma. The symptoms of this illness, whatever its exact diagnosis, only affected Jane physically. According to Edward Austen-Leigh his aunt's 'mind did not share in this decay of the bodily strength' and 'the elasticity of her spirits'[29] enabled to her to keep going. When she felt well enough Jane resumed work on *Persuasion*, as her nephew recalled.

> *Persuasion* was not finished before the middle of August in that year, and the manner in which it was then completed affords proof that neither the critical nor the creative powers of the author were at all impaired. The book had been brought to an end in July ... But her performance did not satisfy her. She thought it tame and flat, and was desirous of producing something better. This weighed upon her mind, the more so probably on account of the weak state of her health; so that one night she retired to rest in very low spirits. But such depression was little in accordance with her nature, and was soon shaken off. The next morning she awoke to more cheerful views and brighter inspirations: the sense of power revived; and imagination resumed its course. She cancelled the condemned chapter, and wrote two others, entirely different, in its stead.[30]

In the summer of 1816 Jane was surrounded by many members of her close family. Charles was then staying at Chawton Cottage and Henry was frequently there too. Frank, or 'sweet amiable Frank' as Jane called him, and his family lived at Alton, not far from Anna and her family. The proximity of her loved ones must have been a comfort to Jane as her health deteriorated.

In August Cassandra accompanied James's wife Mary, who was also unwell, on a trip to Cheltenham. Edward stayed at Chawton Cottage to keep his aunt company while Cassandra was away. On 4 September Jane wrote a cheerful letter to her sister, saying, 'We go on very well here, Edward is a great pleasure to me; – he drove me to Alton yesterday.'[31]

In her next letter, the last one she ever wrote to Cassandra, Jane informed her that 'our day at Alton was very pleasant ... Thank you, my Back has given me scarcely any pain for many days. – I have an idea that agitation does it as much harm as fatigue, & that I was ill at the time of your going, from the very circumstance of your going. – I am nursing myself up now into as beautiful a state as I can, because I hear that Dr White means to call on me before he leaves the Country.'[32]

Jane continued, at times, to be lost in her imaginary world. While Edward was at Chawton, she told him what happened to the main characters of her published novels after the books ended. Edward, like his sisters, was also trying to write a novel and he and Jane read it together. In a lively letter, which Jane wrote to her nephew after he returned home, she made an interesting comparison between their different styles of writing. Referring to part of Edward's manuscript, which had gone missing, Jane wrote,

Two Chapters & a half to be missing is monstrous! It is well that *I* have not been at Steventon lately, & therefore cannot be suspected of purloining them; – two strong twigs & a half towards a Nest of my own, would have been something. – I do not think however that any theft of that sort would be really very useful to me. What should I do with your strong, manly, spirited Sketches, full of Variety and Glow? – How could I possibly join them on to the little bit (two Inches wide) of Ivory on which I work with so fine a Brush, as produces little effect after much labour?[33]

Jane suggested to Edward that they should get 'hold of one or two' of her brother Henry's 'very superior sermons'[34] to put into their novels. Soon after this letter was written Henry was appointed curate of Chawton.

12

THE LAST MONTHS

Two cheerful and hopeful letters written by Jane in early 1817 suggest that she was feeling better. In a letter to her niece Caroline, dated 23 January, she wrote, '*I feel myself getting stronger than I was a half year ago, & can so perfectly well walk to Alton, or back again, without the slightest fatigue that I hope to be able to do both when Summer comes.*'[1]

The following day Jane wrote to her friend Alethea Bigg, saying, '*I have certainly gained strength through the Winter & am not far from being well; & I think I understand my own case now so much better than I did, as to be able by care to keep off any serious return of illness.*'[2]

Jane was well enough at the end of the month to start writing a new novel. The story was set in a seaside resort called Sanditon, which was the name later given by her family to this unfinished novel. William and Richard Austen-Leigh wrote the following paragraphs about this new work:

Jane felt well enough to set to work on a fresh novel: thoroughly fresh, for it bore no resemblance to any of her previous stories ... the scene is laid at a new watering-place, which is being exploited by two of the leading characters. In the twelve chapters which she wrote, the dramatis personae are sketched in with vigour and decision; but there is little of the subtle refinement which we are accustomed to associate with her work, and certainly nothing of the tender sentiment of *Persuasion*.

It is unfair, however, to judge from the first draft of a few introductory chapters, written as they no doubt were to relieve the tedium of long hours of confinement, and written perhaps also to comfort her friends by letting them see that she was still able to work. It is probable, too, that a long step in the downward progress of her condition was taken in the course of the seven weeks during which she was writing for the last time. It began in her usual firm and neat hand, but some of the latter pages were first traced in pencil probably, when she was too ill to sit long at a desk and afterwards written over in ink.[3]

By this time Jane had taken to riding about in a donkey carriage when she was too tired to walk, and had given up her household duties. She needed to take frequent rests. Caroline Austen recalled that, despite her tiredness, Jane refused to monopolise the sofa at Chawton Cottage.

In my later visits to Chawton Cottage, I remember Aunt Jane used often to lie down after dinner – My Grandmother herself was frequently on the sofa – sometimes in the afternoon, sometimes in the evening, at no fixed period of the day, – She had not bad health for her age, and she worked often for hours in the garden, and naturally wanted rest afterwards – There was only one sofa in the room – and Aunt Jane laid upon 3 chairs which she arranged for herself – I think she had a pillow, but it never looked comfortable – She called it *her* sofa, and even when the *other* was unoccupied, *she* never took it – It seemed understood that she preferred the chairs –

I wondered and wondered – for the real sofa was frequently vacant, and *still* she laid in this comfortless manner –I often asked her how she *could* like the chairs best – and I suppose I worried her into telling me the reason of her choice – which was, that if she ever used the sofa, Grandmama would be leaving it for her, and would not lie down, as she did now, whenever she felt inclined.[4]

Fanny Knight sent Jane a number of amusing letters to cheer her up. Three lively letters written in reply show that, despite her illness, Jane remained interested in the lives of those around her. The rapid deterioration in Jane's health is evident in these letters. On 20 to 21 February she wrote, 'I am almost entirely cured of my rheumatism; just a little pain in my knee now & then, to make me remember what it was, & keep on flannel – Aunt Cassandra nursed me so beautifully.'[5]

Jane may have dismissed her illness as only rheumatism to save her family from worry. Her next letter to Fanny, written on 13 March, also sounded quite hopeful. 'I am got tolerably well again, quite equal to walking about & enjoying the Air; & by sitting down & resting a good while between my Walks, I get exercise enough. – I have a scheme however for accomplishing more, as the weather grows springlike. I mean to take to riding the Donkey. It will be more independant (*sic*) & less troublesome than the use of the Carriage, & I shall be able to go about with At Cassandra in her walks to Alton & Wyards.'[6]

Despite the positive tone of these letters, Jane was no longer well enough to write her novel; she wrote the last sentence on 17 March. In her letter to Fanny dated 23 March, although Jane claimed to be feeling better, the alarming symptoms she described indicate that her health was deteriorating rapidly.

Many thanks for your kind care for my health; I certainly have not been well for many weeks, & about a week ago I was very poorly, I have had a good deal of fever at times & indifferent nights, but am considerably better now, & recovering my Looks a little, which have been bad enough, black & white & every wrong colour. I must not depend upon being ever very blooming again. Sickness is a dangerous Indulgence at my time of Life ... I took my 1st ride yesterday & liked it very much. I went up Mounters Lane, & round by where the new Cottages are to be, & found the exercise & everything very pleasant, & I had the advantage of agreable (*sic*) companions, as At Cass: & Edward walked by my side. – At Cass: is such an excellent Nurse, so assiduous & unwearied: But you know all that already.[7]

At the end of March, Jane's uncle, James Leigh-Perrot, died at his home in Berkshire. Mrs Austen, who had been close to her brother, was shocked to discover that he had made no immediate provision for her and her children in his will. According to William and Richard Austen-Leigh this caused Jane's family some distress.

As Jane was affected by anything that affected her nearest relations, we must probably attribute to it some share in the rapid decay of her bodily strength. Her uncle, Mr Leigh Perrot, died at Scarlets (his Berkshire home) on March 28th. He was childless, and left a considerable fortune. As he was also a kind-hearted man and had always shown particular favour to the Austens, it was reasonably expected that they would reap some immediate benefit under his will. Most of the family were in narrow circumstances, and they had lately been crippled by the failure of Henry's business and the lawsuit about Edward's Hampshire property; a legacy, therefore, would have been very acceptable.

Mr Leigh Perrot, however, was actuated in making his will by a stronger motive than love to sister and nephews. He was devoted to his wife, and was perhaps anxious to show that his devotion was increased in consequence of the false accusation with which she had been assailed at Bath in 1799–1800.

He showed it by leaving everything to her for her life, and placing Scarlets and a considerable sum at her free disposal. At the same time he left a large sum (subject to her life interest) to James Austen and his heirs, and 1000 apiece to each of Mrs Austen's children who should survive his wife. Mrs Leigh Perrot, also, at a later date, gave allowances to some members of the family, and eventually made Edward Austen (Jane's nephew) her heir. None of these advantages, however, fell to them immediately.[8]

Mrs Austen's financial circumstances had worsened recently because Frank could no longer afford to give her an allowance, due to the needs of his ever-increasing family, and Henry had also stopped his allowance when he became bankrupt. Jane's distress over her uncle's will, which was made worse by the absence of Cassandra, who was in Berkshire comforting her aunt, brought on a relapse of her illness. The following paragraph, from a letter Jane wrote to her brother Charles on 6 April, shows how badly she was affected.

> I have really been too unwell the last fortnight to write anything that was not absolutely necessary. I have been suffering from a Bilious attack, attended with a good deal of fever. – A few days ago my complaint appeared removed, but I am ashamed to say that the shock of my Uncle's Will brought on a relapse, & I was so ill on Friday & thought myself so likely to be worse that I could not but press for Cassandra's returning with Frank after the Funeral last night, which she of course did, & either

her return, or my having seen Mr Curtis, or my Disorder's chusing (*sic*) to go away, have made me better this morning. I live upstairs however for the present & am coddled. I am the only one of the Legatees who has been so silly, but a weak Body must excuse weak Nerves.[9]

It was in April that Caroline Austen last saw her aunt, as she later recalled.

It had been settled that about the end of (March), or the beginning of April, I should spend a few days at Chawton, in the absence of my Father and Mother, who were just then engaged with Mrs Leigh-Perrot in arranging her late husband's affairs – it was shortly after Mr Leigh-Perrot's death – but Aunt Jane became too ill to have me in the house, and so I went instead to my sister's, Mrs Lefroy, at Wyards – The next day we walked over to Chawton to make enquiries after our Aunt – She was keeping her room but said she would see us, and we went up to her – She was in her dressing gown and was sitting quite like an invalide (*sic*) in an arm chair – but she got up, and kindly greeted us – and then pointing to seats which had been arranged for us by the fire, she said, 'There's a chair for the married lady, and a little stool for you, Caroline.' It is strange, but those trifling words are the last of her's that I can remember – for I retain *no* recollection *at* all of what was said by any one in the conversation that of course ensued – I was struck by the alteration in herself – She was very pale – her voice was weak and low and there was about her, a general appearance of debility and suffering; but I have been told that she never *had* much actual pain – She was not equal to the exertion of talking to us, and our visit to the sick room was a very short one – Aunt Cassandra soon taking us away – I do not suppose we stayed a quarter of an hour; and I never saw Aunt Jane again.[10]

Jane knew that death was approaching because on 27 April she wrote her will, leaving her estate to Cassandra with the exception of a bequest of £50 to Henry. She also left £50 to Henry's housekeeper, as compensation for some money she had lost when Henry's bank failed. The will was not witnessed, probably to spare her family the anguish of knowing that she was sorting out her affairs.

The following month Jane agreed to go to Winchester with Cassandra, to seek the help of Giles King Lyford, the Surgeon-in-Ordinary at Winchester Hospital. Jane described her journey in a letter to her nephew Edward dated 27 May: 'Thanks to the kindness of your Father & Mother in sending me their Carriage, my Journey hither on Saturday was performed with very little fatigue, & had it been a fine day, I think I shd have felt none, but it distressed me to see Uncle Henry & Wm K., who kindly attended us on horseback, riding in the rain almost all the way.'[11]

Jane's friends Alethea Bigg and Elizabeth Heathcote found comfortable lodgings for her at 8 College Street, just behind the cathedral. According to Edward Austen-Leigh, Jane's friends did all they could to help 'both by their society, and by supplying those little conveniences in which a lodging-house was likely to be deficient'.[12] Jane was constantly attended by Cassandra, whom she described as 'my dearest sister, my tender, watchful, indefatigable nurse'.[13] James and Henry visited their sister regularly, and administered holy communion to her. In her last surviving letter, dated 28 to 29 May, which was written to a friend in London, Jane acknowledged the debt she owed to Cassandra and the rest of her family. 'As to what I to owe her, and to the anxious affection of all my beloved family on this occasion, I can only cry over it, and pray God to bless them more and more.'

This letter also showed how brave and resigned Jane was. 'But I am getting too near complaint. It has been the appointment of God, however secondary causes may have operated...'[14]

In his *Biographical Notice*, Henry Austen described how cheerful and courageous Jane remained, in spite of her suffering. 'She supported, during two months, all the varying pain, irksomeness, and tedium, attendant on decaying nature, with more than resignation, with a truly elastic cheerfulness.'[15]

Despite his renowned skills, Mr Lyford could not give any hope of a recovery. According to Edward Austen-Leigh, 'Mr Lyford spoke encouragingly. It was not, of course, his business to extinguish hope in his patient, but I believe that he had, from the first, very little expectation of a permanent cure. All that was gained by the removal from home was the satisfaction of having done the best that could be done, together with such alleviations of suffering as superior medical skill could afford.'[16]

On 6 June Mary Austen, James's wife, went to Winchester to help Cassandra with nursing. According to Caroline Austen, Jane 'suddenly ... became much worse – Mr Lyford thought the end was near at hand, and she beleived (*sic*) *herself* to be dying – and under this conviction she said all that she wished to say to those around her. In taking then, as she thought, a last leave of my Mother, she thanked her for being there, and said, "You have always been a kind sister to me, Mary."'[17]

Charles Austen, who had been ill himself, arrived just as Jane was emerging from this crisis. Frank, whose wife had recently given birth to her seventh child and needed him at home, was not able to visit her at all.

Jane recovered enough to raise hopes that she might be granted a respite from death. Mrs Austen reported to her granddaughter Anna that Jane was sleeping better and feeling more comfortable, but this did not last long. Jane remained sound in mind until the end, however, with her sense of humour and fun intact. On 15 July Jane composed her final piece of writing, a witty poem about St Swithin's Day.

Jane's last days were described in detail in the following letter, written on 20 July, by Cassandra to her niece Fanny Knight.

My dearest Fanny – doubly dear to me now for her dear sake whom we have lost.

She *did* love you most sincerely, & never shall I forget the proofs of love you gave her during her illness in writing those kind, amusing letters at a time when I know your feelings would have dictated so different a style. Take the only reward I can give you in my assurance that your benevolent purpose *was* answer'd, you *did* contribute to her enjoyment. Even your last letter afforded pleasure, I merely cut the seal & gave it to her, she opened it & read it herself, afterwards she gave it me to read & then talked to me a little & not unchearfully (*sic*) of its contents, but there was then a languor about her which prevented her taking the same interest in any thing, she had been used to do. Since Tuesday evening, when her complaint returnd, there was a visible change, she slept more & much more comfortably, indeed during the last eight & forty hours she was more asleep than awake. Her looks altered & she fell away, but I perceived no material diminution of strength & tho' I was then hopeless of a recovery I had no suspicion how rapidly my loss was approaching. – I *have* lost a treasure, such a Sister, such a friend as never can have been surpassed, – She was the sun of my life, the gilder of every pleasure, the soother of every sorrow, I had not a thought concealed from her, & it is as if I had lost a part of myself. I loved her only too well, not better than she deserved, but I am conscious that my affection for her made me sometimes unjust to & negligent of others, & I can acknowledge, more than as a general principle, the justice of the hand which has struck this blow. You know me too well to be at all afraid that I should suffer materially from my feelings, I am perfectly conscious of the extent of my irreparable loss, but I am not at all overpowerd & very little indisposed, nothing but what a short time, with rest & change of air will remove. I thank God that I was enabled to attend her to the last & amongst my many causes of self-reproach I have not to add any wilfull (*sic*) neglect of her comfort. She felt herself to be dying about half an hour before she became tranquil & aparently (*sic*) unconscious. During that half hour was her struggle, poor Soul! she said she could not tell us what she sufferd, tho' she complaind of little fixed pain. When I asked her if there was anything she wanted, her answer was she wanted nothing but death & some of her words were, 'God grant me patience, Pray for me Oh Pray for me.' Her voice was affected but as long as she spoke she was intelligible. I hope I do not break your heart my dearest Fanny by these particulars, I mean to afford you gratification whilst I am relieving my own feelings. I could not write so to anybody else, indeed you are the only person I have written to at all excepting your Grandmama, it was to her not your Uncle Charles I wrote on Friday. – Immediately after dinner on Thursday I went into the Town to do an errand which your dear Aunt was anxious about. I returnd about a quarter before six & found her recovering from faintness & oppression, she got so well as to be able to give me a minute account of her seisure (*sic*) & when the clock struck 6 she was talking quietly to me. I cannot say how soon afterwards she was seized again with the same faintness, which was followed by the sufferings she could not describe, but Mr Lyford had been sent for, had applied something to give her ease & she was in a state of quiet insensibility by seven oclock at the latest. From that time till half past four when she ceased to breathe, she scarcely moved a limb, so that we have every reason to think, with gratitude to the Almighty, that her sufferings were over. A slight motion of the head with every breath remaind till almost the last. I sat close to her with a pillow in my lap to assist in supporting her head, which was almost off the bed, for six hours, – fatigue made me then resign my place to Mrs J. A. for two hours & a half when I took it again & in about one hour more she breathed her last. I was able to close her eyes myself & it was a great gratification to me to render her these last services. There was nothing convulsed or which gave the idea of pain in her look, on the contrary, but for the continual motion of the head, she gave me the idea of a beautiful statue, & even now in her coffin, there is such a sweet serene air over her countenance as is quite pleasant to contemplate. This day my dearest Fanny you have had the melancholly (*sic*) intelligence & I know you suffer severely, but I likewise know that you will apply to the fountain-head for consolation & that our merciful God is never deaf to such prayers as you will offer.

The last sad ceremony is to take place on Thursday morning, her dear remains are to be deposited in the Cathedral – it is a satisfaction to me to think that they are to lie in a Building she admired so much – her precious soul I presume to hope reposes in a far superior Mansion. May mine one day be reunited to it. – Your dear Papa, your Uncles Henry & Frank & Edwd Austen instead of his Father will attend, I hope they will none of them suffer lastingly from their pious exertions. – The ceremony must be over before ten o'clock as the Cathedral service begins at that hour, so that we shall be at home early in the day, for there will be nothing to keep us here afterwards. – Your Uncle James came to us yesterday & is gone home to day – Uncle H. goes to Chawton tomorrow morning, he has given every necessary direction here & I think his company there will do good. He returns to us again on Tuesday evening. I did not think to have written a long letter when I began, but I have found the employment draw me on & I hope I shall have been giving you more pleasure than pain…

Most affectly yrs

Cass. Elizth Austen[18]

It was not customary for women to attend funerals in the early nineteenth century, so Cassandra did not accompany her sister's body on its final journey. She described her last sight of the funeral procession in another letter to her niece, written on 28 July, after she had returned to Chawton to comfort her grieving mother.

> Thursday was not so dreadful a day to me as you imagined, there was so much necessary to be done that there was not time for additional misery. Every thing was conducted with the greatest tranquillity, & but that I was determined I would see the last & therefore was upon the listen, I should not have known when they left the House. I watched the little mournful procession the length of the Street & when it turned from my sight & I had lost her for ever – even then I was not overpowered, nor so much agitated as I am now in writing of it.[19]

It was probably connections of Jane's clergyman brothers who arranged for her to be buried in Winchester Cathedral. The inscription on her grave reads,

> In Memory of
> JANE AUSTEN
> youngest daughter of the late
> Revd. GEORGE AUSTEN
> formerly Rector of Steventon in this County
> she departed this Life on the 18th July 1817,
> aged 41, after a long illness supported with
> the patience and hopes of a Christian.
>
> The benevolence of her heart,
> the sweetness of her temper, and
> the extraordinary endowments of her mind

obtained the regard of all who knew her, and
the warmest love of her intimate connections.
Their grief is in proportion to their affection,
they know their loss to be irreparable,
but in their deepest affliction they are consoled
by a firm though humble hope that her charity,
devotion, faith and purity, have rendered
her soul acceptable in the sight of her
REDEEMER

Although the inscription makes reference to the 'extraordinary endowments' of Jane's mind, no mention is made of the fact that she was an author. When the inscription was written, Jane had not yet been recognised as the great writer that she was. Jane's family was very proud of her, and not only for her literary achievements, as recorded in the final paragraph of Caroline Austen's *Memoir*. 'I need scarcely say she was dearly loved by her family – Her Brothers were very proud of her – Her literary fame, at the close of her life, was only just spreading – but they were proud of her talents, which *they* even then estimated highly – proud of her home virtues, of her cheerful spirit – of her pleasant looks – and *each* loved afterwards to *fancy* a resemblance in some daughter of his own, to the dear Aunt Jane, whose perfect equal they *yet* never expected to see.'[20]

13

GROWING FAME

Henry acted as Jane's literary executor. One of the first things he did was to prepare her two unpublished novels for the press. To the first novel Jane wrote, which she had called *Susan*, he gave the name *Northanger Abbey*, and to her final novel he gave the name *Persuasion*. These novels were published together by John Murray, in a four-volume edition, at the end of 1817. As with Jane's other works, her name did not appear on the title page, but Henry included a 'Biographical Notice' in which he identified her as the author of all six of her novels. *Northanger Abbey* was prefaced by an 'Advertisement By the Authoress' which Jane had written after Henry recovered the manuscript from Richard Crosby. This read as follows:

This little work was finished in the year 1803 and intended for immediate publication. It was disposed of to a bookseller, it was even advertised, and why the business proceeded no farther, the author has never been able to learn. That any bookseller should think it worth while to purchase what he did not think it worth while to publish seems extraordinary. But with this, neither the author nor the public have any other concern than as some observation is necessary upon those parts of the work which thirteen years have made comparatively obsolete. The public are entreated to bear in mind that thirteen years have passed since it was finished, many more since it was begun, and that during that period, places, manners, books, and opinions have undergone considerable changes.

In 1832 the publisher Richard Bentley bought the copyright of all Jane's novels, except *Pride and Prejudice*, from Cassandra and Henry Austen for £250. He then bought the copyright of *Pride and Prejudice* from the executors of Thomas Egerton, to whom Jane had sold it. The six novels were published by Bentley in 1833, in his series of one-volume 'Standard Novels'. This edition included a *Memoir of Miss Austen* by Henry, which was a revised and extended version of his *Biographical Notice* of 1817. Bentley also included an *Editorial Paragraph* in which he claimed that Jane was 'the founder of a school of novelists' who had broken free from the influence of her contemporary writers, and 'with combined boldness and modesty struck into a path of her own, of which she remains to this day, the undisputed mistress'. He went on to describe Jane as 'emphatically the novelist of home'.[1]

Jane's novels were reprinted several times over the thirty years after Bentley's edition was published. However, despite the recognition of her genius by Bentley and others, her fame increased only gradually. In the words of her nephew Edward,

Seldom has any literary reputation been of such slow growth as that of Jane Austen ... To the multitude her works appeared tame and commonplace, poor in colouring, and sadly deficient in incident and interest. It is true that we were sometimes cheered by hearing that a different verdict had been pronounced by more competent judges; we were told how some great statesman or distinguished poet held these works in high estimation; we had the satisfaction of believing that they were most admired by the best judges … But though such golden opinions were now and then gathered in, yet the wide field of public taste yielded no adequate return either in praise or profit. Her reward was not to be the quick return of the cornfield, but the slow growth of the tree which is to endure to another generation.[2]

In the early Victorian period Jane's novels were not as popular as the passionate works of Charlotte Bronte, or the social novels of Mrs Gaskell and Charles Dickens. Her novels were seen by many as superficial, and Jane herself was regarded as rather prim, cold and prudish. However, in time, Jane's reputation grew. According to her brother Henry, the 'merit' of her eventually being recognised as a great writer belonged 'less to reviewers than the general readers'.[3] In the words of Edward Austen-Leigh, 'The public taste was forming itself all this time, and grew by what it fed on.' He also pointed out that his aunt's novels belonged 'to a class which gain rather than lose by frequent perusals'.[4]

In the 1860s there occurred what William and Richard Austen-Leigh described as 'the beginning of a great advance in her fame'.[5] Soon Jane's readers wanted to know more about her life and character. People also began to flock to her grave in Winchester Cathedral, which led to a puzzled verger enquiring, 'Is there anything particular about that lady?' Around this time Jane's nephew decided to write his biography of her. This was partly because Jane's last surviving sibling had died in 1865, and it was felt the time had come to record family memories of her. As Caroline Austen wrote in 1867, 'The generation who knew her is passing away – but those who are succeeding us must feel an interest in the personal character of their Great Aunt, who has made the family name in some small degree, illustrious.'[6]

Another reason for writing a biography was that, with Jane's growing reputation and popularity, someone outside the family may attempt to do so. Edward, therefore, set to work and *A Memoir of Jane Austen and Other Family Recollections* was published in 1869. This biography portrayed Jane as a kind and much-loved daughter, sister and aunt, as well as a talented writer. Following its publication Edward was pleased and surprised to receive letters from strangers in England and America. According to his daughter, 'he had not realised to how large a number of readers, and in what a high degree, the aunt to whom he as a boy and young man had been so warmly attached, had also become a living, though an unseen friend'.[7]

Due to this overwhelming response, a second extended edition of the *Memoir* was published in 1871. This edition included Jane's early work *Lady Susan*, her unfinished novel *The Watsons*, a synopsis of *Sanditon*, the cancelled chapter of *Persuasion* and a few letters. In his preface Edward wrote, 'The memoir of my Aunt, Jane Austen, has been received with more favour than I had ventured to expect. The notices taken of it in the periodical press, as well as letters addressed to me by many with whom I am not personally acquainted, show that an unabated interest is still taken in every particular that can be told about her. I am thus encouraged not only to offer a Second Edition of the Memoir, but also to enlarge it with some additional matter which I might have scrupled to intrude on the public if they had not thus seemed to call for it.'

The success of the *Memoir* led to a reissue of the novels, including colour-illustrated and collectors' editions. The profits from the book paid for the making of a memorial brass tablet to Jane, which was placed near her grave in 1872. By this time, no-one needed to ask if there was 'anything particular' about the lady buried in the north aisle of Winchester Cathedral. The inscription on the tablet reads

JANE AUSTEN
Known to many by her

writings, endeared to
her family by the
varied charms of her
Character and ennobled
by Christian faith
and piety, was born
at Steventon in the
County of Hants Dec.
xvi mdcclxxv, and buried
in this Cathedral
July xxiv mdcccxvii
'She openeth her
mouth with wisdom
and in her tongue is
the law of kindness'
Prov.x xxi .v.xxvi

In 1884 Jane's great-nephew Lord Brabourne, Fanny Knight's son, published a large number of letters he had inherited from the Austen and Knight families. This two-volume edition of the letters was accompanied by a biographical essay and a commentary on the novels.

The appetite for Jane's works and the interest in her life continued into the twentieth century. In 1900 a memorial window, paid for by public subscription, was placed in the window of Winchester Cathedral above the mural tablet. It bears an inscription in Latin which translates as 'Remember in the Lord, Jane Austen who died July 18 A.D.1817'.

By this time Jane's novels had become the subject of academic and critical studies. She was recognised as having made the novel as important a literary form as drama and poetry. At the same time the novels continued to appeal to readers, of both sexes, who wanted an enjoyable, readable story to escape into. To satisfy the ongoing interest in Jane's life, two more family biographies were written. In 1913 William and Richard Austen-Leigh published *Jane Austen, Her Life and Times, A Family Record*, and in 1920 Mary Augusta Austen-Leigh published *Personal Aspects of Jane Austen*. In 1947, Chawton Cottage was turned into a museum dedicated to Jane.

In the twentieth century Jane's reputation reached cult status. Her works were translated into numerous languages and achieved a worldwide readership. They also became the subject of study in schools and universities. Sequels to the novels were written and her unfinished works were completed. Jane's novels were read on the radio, acted on stage, televised, and made into award-winning films. A thriving commercial industry was created out of her fame.

There is no sign of Jane's fame and popularity abating in the twenty-first century. Her great nephew, Lord Brabourne, analysed the reasons for her popularity at the end of the nineteenth century, and his analysis is as valid today as it was then.

The popularity continues, although the customs and manners which Jane Austen describes have changed and varied so much as to belong in a great measure to another age. But the reason of its continuance is not far to seek. Human nature is the same in all ages of the world, and 'the inimitable Jane' (as an old friend of mine used always to call her) is true to Nature from first to last. She does not attract our imagination by sensational descriptions or marvellous plots; but with so little 'plot' at all as to offend those who read only for excitement, she describes men and women exactly as men and women really are, and tells her tale of ordinary, everyday life with such truthful delineation, such bewitching simplicity, and, moreover, with such purity of style and language, as have rarely been equalled, and perhaps never surpassed.[8]

Jane would have been astonished to know that the novels, which were originally written to amuse and entertain her family, have achieved such status and worldwide fame, and that she is regarded by some as being second only to Shakespeare in literary importance.

14

OBSERVATIONS & OPINIONS ON THE NOVELS

All of Jane Austen's novels are about life in late Georgian, rural England from the woman's point of view. They all have a domestic setting and can all be described, with the possible exception of *Mansfield Park*, as light-hearted love stories. The characters are mostly drawn from the gentry class of society, but a few come from the classes above and below this level. The heroines of all the stories have to undergo a journey of self-discovery and, having acquired the necessary self-knowledge through a series of lessons or trials, fall in love with and marry the right man.

There are two themes common to all six novels – repentance and the importance of love in marriage. The novels have a moral undertone, but the author is never openly didactic. The reader has to draw his or her own moral conclusions, from the rewards or punishments meted out for good or bad behaviour. In the words of Edward Austen-Leigh, 'they (the novels) certainly were not written to support any theory or inculcate any particular moral, except indeed the great moral which is to be equally gathered from an observation of the course of actual life – namely, the superiority of high over low principles, and of greatness over littleness of mind'.[1]

Jane Austen's novels all have a fairly narrow focus, which she herself described as 'three or four families in a country village'.[2] As a result of this narrow focus, significant events which occurred during the time in which the novels are set, such as the Napoleonic Wars, are only alluded to or appear in the background. The world of the novels is rather a sanitised world, in which issues such as poverty and social unrest hardly feature. This somewhat unbalanced picture is the result of Jane's decision not to 'dwell on guilt and misery',[3] as she explained in her authorial comment in *Mansfield Park*. This sunny world reflects the author's happy and positive personality and, possibly, represents the world she would have liked to live in.

The heroines of the novels are all intelligent, determined characters who regard themselves as equal to men. They are far from the meek and subservient ideal of Georgian womanhood. Although Jane was not an openly feminist writer, she showed, through her fictional characters, how some women fought back against the constraints imposed on them by a patriarchal society.

Each of the novels has a different atmosphere, as Mary Augusta Austen-Leigh pointed out in her biography. 'Every novel is complete in itself, possessing its own plot, characters and distinctive atmosphere in a remarkable degree. We find scarcely any repetition of ideas among the six, and this may induce the belief that while comparison is easy, combination is impossible, as they possess no similarity among themselves apart from the creative, dramatic, humorous qualities common to all.'[4]

Another feature common to all the novels is the brilliant characterisation. Henry Austen described Jane's power of inventing characters as 'intuitive and almost unlimited'.[5] He also wrote,

> The plots are simple in construction, and yet intricate in development; – the main characters, those that the reader feels sure are to love, marry, and make mischief, are introduced in the first or second chapter; the work is all done by half a dozen people; no person, scene, or sentence, is ever introduced needless to the matter in hand:

– no catastrophes, or discoveries, or surprises of a grand nature, are allowed – neither children nor fortunes are lost or found by accident – the mind is never taken off the level surface of life – the reader breakfasts, dines, walks, and gossips, with the various worthies, till a process of transmutation takes place in him, and he absolutely fancies himself one of the company. Yet the winding up of the plot involves a surprise: a few incidents are entangled at the beginning in the most simple and natural manner, and till the close one never feels quite sure how they are to be disentangled. Disentangled, however, they are, and that in a most satisfactory manner.[6]

The Opinions of Some Eminent Writers on Jane Austen and Her Novels

Read again, and for the third time at least, Miss Austen's very finely written novel of *Pride and Prejudice*. That young lady had a talent for describing the involvements and feelings and characters of ordinary life which is to me the most wondrous I have ever met with. The Big Bow-wow strain I can do myself like any now going; but the exquisite touch, which renders ordinary common place things and characters interesting, from the truth of the description and the sentiment, is denied to me. What a pity such a gifted creature died so early.

Sir Walter Scott, 1826

The passions are perfectly unknown to her; she rejects even a speaking acquaintance with that stormy sisterhood ... What sees keenly, speaks aptly, moves flexibly, it suits her to study: but what throbs fast and full, though hidden, what the blood rushes through, what is the unseen seat of life and the sentient target of death – this Miss Austen ignores ... Jane Austen was a complete and most sensible lady, but a very incomplete and rather insensible (not senseless) woman. If this heresy, I cannot help it.

Charlotte Brontë, 1850

First and foremost let Austen be named, the greatest artist that has ever written, using the term to signify the most perfect mastery over the means to her end. There are heights and depths in human nature Miss Austen has never scaled nor fathomed, there are worlds of passionate existence into which she has never set foot: but although this is obvious to every reader, it is equally obvious that she risked no failures by attempting to delineate that which she had not seen. Her circle may be restricted, but it is complete. Her world is a perfect orb, and vital. Life, as it presents itself to an English gentlewoman peacefully yet actively engaged in her quiet village, is mirrored in her works with a purity and fidelity that must endow them with interest for all time.

George Henry Lewes, 1852

I would almost cut off one of my hands, if it would enable me to write like your aunt with the other.

Miss Mitford (addressed to Edward Austen-Leigh), 1869

I am reported to have said that Jane Austen was equal to Shakespeare. What I really said was that, in the narrow sphere of life which she delineated, she pictured her characters as truthfully as Shakespeare. But Austen is to Shakespeare as asteroid to sun. Miss Austen's novels are perfect works on small scale – beautiful bits of stippling.

Alfred Lord Tennyson, 1870

Jane lies in Winchester – blessed be her shade!
Praise the Lord for making her, and her for all she made!
And while the stones of Winchester, or Milsom Street, remain
Glory, love, and honour, unto England's Jane.

Rudyard Kipling, 1924

The balance of her gifts was singularly perfect. Among her finished novels there were no failures, and, among her chapters few that sink markedly below the level of the others … the most perfect artist among women, the writer whose books are immortal, died just as she was beginning to feel confident in her own success … Jane Austen is thus a mistress of much deeper emotion than appears upon the surface … always the stress is laid upon character.

Virginia Woolf, 1925

Most works in realism tell a succession of such abject truths; they are deeply in earnest, every detail is true, and yet the whole finally tumbles to the ground – true but without significance.

How did Jane Austen save her novels from that danger? They appear to be compact of abject truth. Their events are excruciatingly unimportant, and yet, with *R. Crusoe*, they will probably outlast all Fielding, Scott, George Eliot, Thackeray and Dickens. The art is so consummate that the secret is hidden: peer at them as hard as one may; shake them; take them apart; one cannot see how it is done.

Thornton Wilder, 1938

If I were in doubt as to the wisdom of one of my actions I should not consult Flaubert or Dostoyevsky. The opinion of Balzac or Dickens would carry little weight with me. Were Stendhal to rebuke me, it would only convince me I had done right; even in the judgement of Tolstoy I should not put complete confidence. But I should be seriously upset, I should worry for weeks and weeks, if I incurred the disapproval of Jane Austen.

Lord David Cecil, 1949

NOTES

1. Childhood 1775–1786

1. Austen-Leigh, William and Richard Arthur, *Jane Austen, Her Life and Letters, A Family Record* (1913), p. 16.

2. Austen-Leigh, J. E., *A Memoir of Jane Austen and Other Family Recollections* (1869), p. 14.

3. Ibid., p. 39.

4. Austen-Leigh, William and Richard Arthur, p. 15.

5. Austen-Leigh, J. E., p. 216.

6. Austen-Leigh, William and Richard Arthur, p. 15.

7. Austen-Leigh, J. E., p. 19.

8. Ibid., p. 39.

9. Austen, Caroline, *My Aunt Jane Austen, A Memoir* (1867), p. 11.

10. Ibid., p. 11.

11. Austen-Leigh, J. E., p. 160.

12. Ibid., p. 19.

13. Austen-Leigh, Mary Augusta, *Personal Aspects of Jane Austen* (1920), p. 54.

14. Austen-Leigh, J. E., p. 23.

15. Ibid., p. 23.

16. Hill, Constance, *Jane Austen, Her Homes and Her Friends* (1923), p. 30.

17. Austen-Leigh, J. E., p. 21.

18. Ibid., p. 23.

19. Ibid., p. 24.

20. Hill, p. 14.

21. Ibid., p. 64.

22. Austen-Leigh, J. E., p. 26.

23. Austen-Leigh, Mary Augusta, p. 9.

24. Austen, Jane, *Emma*, chapter 3.

25. Hill, p. 35.

26. Ibid., p. 37.

27. Ibid., p. 37.

28. Ibid., p. 38.

2. Juvenilia 1787–1793

1. Austen-Leigh, J. E., p. 137.

2. Ibid., p. 141.

3. Austen-Leigh, William and Richard Arthur, p. 19.

4. Austen-Leigh, J. E., p. 39.

5. Austen-Leigh, Mary Augusta, p. 32.

6. Austen-Leigh, J. E., p. 183.

7. Austen, Caroline, p. 7.

8. Austen-Leigh, J. E., p. 139.

9. Hill, p. 30.

10. Austen-Leigh, Mary Augusta, p. 14.

11. Austen-Leigh, J. E., p. 42.

12. Ibid., p. 40.

13. Austen-Leigh, William and Richard Arthur, p. 33.

14. Ibid., p. 33.

15. Ibid., p. 34.

3. The Parson's Daughter 1794–1796

1. Austen-Leigh, J. E., p. 130.

2. Ibid., p. 141.

3. Ibid., p. 32.

4. Hill, p. 53.

5. Austen-Leigh, William and Richard Arthur, p. 13.

6. Ibid., p. 44.

7. Austen, Caroline, p. 9.

8. Austen-Leigh, William and Richard Arthur, p. 44.

9. Le Faye, *Jane Austen's Letters* (1995), p. 1.

10. Ibid., p. 2.

11. Ibid., p. 3.

12. Ibid., p. 4.

13. Austen-Leigh, J. E., p. 48.

14. Ibid., p. 186.

15. Le Faye, p. 8.

16. Austen-Leigh, William and Richard Arthur, p. 27.

4. The Early Writing Period 1797–1800

1. Austen-Leigh, William and Richard Arthur, p. 56.

2. Ibid., p. 56.

3. Austen-Leigh, J. E., p. 158.

4. Ibid., p. 105.

5. Ibid., p. 185.

6. Austen-Leigh, William and Richard Arthur, p. 57.

7. Le Faye, p. 216.

8. Austen-Leigh, William and Richard Arthur, p. 57.

9. Austen-Leigh, Mary Augusta, p. 8.

10. Le Faye, p. 15.

11. Ibid., p. 17.

12. Austen-Leigh, William and

Richard Arthur, p. 45.

13. Ibid., p. 45.

14. Ibid., p. 45.

15. Austen-Leigh, W. and R. A., and Le Faye, Deirdre, *Jane Austen, A Family Record* (1989), p. 32.

16. Ibid., p. 97.

17. Le Faye, p. 19.

18. Austen, Caroline, p. 5.

19. Le Faye, p. 29.

20. Ibid., p. 33.

21. Ibid., p. 35.

22. Hill, p. 76.

23. Le Faye, p. 39.

24. Ibid., p. 42.

25. Ibid., p. 43.

26. Ibid., p. 45.

27. Ibid., p. 47.

28. Austen-Leigh, William and Richard Arthur, p. 71.

29. Le Faye, p. 31.

30. Austen-Leigh, J. E., p. 148.

31. Ibid., p. 19.

32. Le Faye, p. 64.

5. Bath 1801–1802

1. Austen-Leigh, William and Richard Arthur, p. 82.

2. Le Faye, p. 68.

3. Ibid., p. 76.

4. Hill, p. 94.

5. Le Faye, pp. 81–2.

6. Ibid., p. 82.

7. Hill, p. 97.

8. Ibid., p. 109.

9. Le Faye, p. 84.

10. Ibid., p. 85.

11. Hill, p. 122.

12. Ibid., p. 104.

13. Austen-Leigh, J. E., p. 29.

14. Austen-Leigh, W. and R. A., and Le Faye, Deirdre, p. 120.

15. Ibid., p. 120.

16. Austen-Leigh, J. E., p. 29.

17. Austen-Leigh, W. and R. A., and Le Faye, Deirdre, p. 122.

6. Bath 1803–1805

1. Austen-Leigh, W. and R. A. and Le Faye, Deirdre, p. 124.

2. Austen-Leigh, Mary Augusta, p. 29.

3. Austen-Leigh, William and Richard Arthur, p. 92.

4. Austen-Leigh, Mary Augusta, p. 29.

5. Austen-Leigh, William and Richard Arthur, p.2.

6. Hill, p. 134.

7. Le Faye, p. 152.

8. Ibid., p. 95.

9. Ibid., pp. 97–8.

7. From Bath to Southampton 1805–1809

1. Austen-Leigh, William and

Richard Arthur, p. 101.

2. Austen-Leigh, W. and R. A. and Le Faye, Deirdre, p. 139.

3. Austen-Leigh, J. E., p. 66.

4. Le Faye, p. 119.

5. Ibid., p. 119.

6. Austen-Leigh, William and Richard Arthur, p. 103.

7. Le Faye, p. 117.

8. Ibid., p. 119.

9. Hill, p. 178.

10. Austen-Leigh, W. and R. A., and Le Faye, Deirdre, p. 144.

11. Ibid., p. 147.

12. Le Faye, p. 125.

13. Ibid., p. 144.

14. Ibid., p. 127.

15. Ibid., p. 136.

16. Ibid., p. 129.

17. Ibid., p. 147.

18. Ibid., p. 150.

19. Ibid., p. 163.

20. Austen-Leigh, J. E., p. 67.

21. Le Faye, p. 156.

22. Ibid., p. 174.

23. Ibid., p. 175.

8. Chawton 1809–1810

1. Le Faye, p. 161.

2. Austen-Leigh, J. E., p. 67.

3. Hill, p. 170.

4. Austen, Caroline, p. 3.

5. Ibid., p. 4.

6. Austen-Leigh, J. E., p. 213.

7. Austen, Caroline, p. 6.

8. Ibid., pp. 6–8.

9. Austen-Leigh, J. E., p. 193.

10. Austen-Leigh, William and Richard Arthur, p. 123.

11. Ibid., p. 126.

12. Austen-Leigh, J. E., p. 81.

13. Ibid., p. 81.

14. Ibid., p. 149.

15. Le Faye, pp. 177–8.

16. Austen-Leigh, J. E., p. 10.

17. Ibid., p. 157.

18. Austen, Caroline, p. 5.

19. Austen-Leigh, William and Richard Arthur, p. 126.

20. Austen-Leigh, J. E., p. xlvi.

21. Austen, Caroline, p. 5.

22. Austen-Leigh, J. E., p. 70.

23. Ibid., p. 139.

24. Ibid., p. 160.

25. Ibid., p. 79.

26. Ibid., p. 79.

27. Austen-Leigh, Mary Augusta, p. 18.

9. The Later Writing Period 1811–1812

1. Austen-Leigh, J. E., p. 82.

2. Le Faye, p. 182.

3. Ibid., p. 182.

4. Ibid., p. 179.

5. Ibid., p. 179.

6. Ibid., p. 183.

7. Austen-Leigh, William and Richard Arthur, p. 132.

8. Austen-Leigh, W. and R. A. and Le Faye, Deirdre, p. 166.

9. Ibid., p. 168.

10. Austen-Leigh, William and Richard Arthur, p. 133.

11. Ibid., p. 123.

12. Ibid., p. 133.

13. Hill, p. 194.

14. Austen-Leigh, W. and R. A., and Le Faye, Deirdre, p. 170.

15. Ibid., p. 171.

16. Le Faye, p. 197.

17. Austen-Leigh, J. E., p. 149.

10. The Later Writing Period 1813–1814

1. Le Faye, p. 201.

2. Ibid., p. 201.

3. Austen-Leigh, William and Richard Arthur, p. 134.

4. Austen-Leigh, W. and R. A., and Le Faye, Deirdre, p. 174.

5. Ibid., p. 175.

6. Ibid., p. 175.

7. Austen-Leigh, J. E., p. 149.

8. Le Faye, p. 205.

9. Austen-Leigh, W. and R. A. and Le Faye, Deirdre, p. 178.

10. Austen-Leigh, William and Richard Arthur, p. 138.

11. Le Faye, p. 212.

12. Ibid., p. 213.

13. Ibid., p. 215.

14. Ibid., p. 217.

15. Ibid., p. 231.

16. Ibid., p. 231.

17. Austen-Leigh, W. and R. A. and Le Faye, Deirdre, p. 180.

18. Le Faye, p. 224.

19. Ibid., p. 230.

20. Ibid., p. 226.

21. Ibid., p. 253.

22. Ibid., p. 251.

23. Hill, p. 202.

24. Austen-Leigh, W. and R. A., and Le Faye, Deirdre, p. 184.

25. Ibid., p. 25.

26. Austen-Leigh, J. E., p. 149.

27. Austen-Leigh, William and Richard Arthur, p. 159.

28. Le Faye, p. 255.

29. Ibid., p. 258.

30. Ibid., p. 261.

31. Austen-Leigh, W. and R. A., and Le Faye, Deirdre, p. 189.

32. Ibid., p. 190.

33. Austen-Leigh, William and Richard Arthur, p. 157.

34. Ibid., p. 157.

35. Austen-Leigh, J. E., p. 118.

36. Le Faye, p. 267.

37. Ibid., p. 275.

38. Ibid., p. 284.

39. Ibid., p. 279.
40. Ibid., p. 280.
41. Ibid., p. 286.
42. Ibid., p. 285.
43. Austen-Leigh, J. E., p. 79.

11. The Later Writing Period 1815–16
1. Austen, Caroline, p. 5.
2. Ibid., p. 6.
3. Ibid., p. 10.
4. Ibid., p. 6.
5. Le Faye, p. 291.
6. Ibid., p. 293.
7. Austen-Leigh, J. E., p. 91.
8. Le Faye, p. 299.
9. Ibid., p. 296.
10. Ibid., p. 306.
11. Ibid., p. 311.
12. Ibid., p. 312.
13. Austen, Caroline, p. 12.
14. Austen-Leigh, W. and R. A., and Le Faye, Deirdre, p. 207.
15. Ibid., p. 207.
16. Austen-Leigh, J. E., p. 117.
17. Ibid., p. 118.
18. Ibid., p. 118.
19. Ibid., p. 118.
20. Austen-Leigh, W. and R. A., and Le Faye, Deirdre, p. 209.
21. Ibid., p. 209.
22. Le Faye, p. 310.
23. Hill, p. 230.

24. Austen-Leigh, J. E., p. 138.
25. Austen-Leigh, William and Richard Arthur, p. 172.
26. Ibid., p. 172.
27. Austen, Caroline, p. 14.
28. Austen-Leigh, J. E., p. 124.
29. Ibid., p. 124.
30. Ibid., p. 124.
31. Le Faye, p. 318.
32. Ibid., p. 320.
33. Le Faye, p. 323.
34. Ibid., p. 323.

12. The Last Months
1. Le Faye, p. 326.
2. Ibid., p. 326.
3. Austen-Leigh, William and Richard Arthur, p. 197.
4. Austen, Caroline, p. 13.
5. Le Faye, p. 329.
6. Ibid., p. 333.
7. Ibid., p. 335.
8. Austen-Leigh, William and Richard Arthur, p. 198.
9. Le Faye, p. 338.
10. Austen-Leigh, W. and R. A., and Le Faye, Deirdre, p. 223.
11. Le Faye, p. 342.
12. Austen-Leigh, J. E., p. 129.
13. Le Faye, p. 343.
14. Ibid., p. 343.
15. Austen-Leigh, J. E., p. 138.
16. Ibid., p. 128.

17. Austen, Caroline, p. 16.

18. Le Faye, p. 343.

19. Ibid., p. 347.

20. Austen, Caroline, p. 17.

13. Growing Fame

1. Austen-Leigh, J. E., p. 154.

2. Ibid., pp. 104–5.

3. Ibid., p. 151.

4. Ibid., p. 109.

5. Austen-Leigh, William and Richard Arthur, p. 208.

6. Austen, Caroline, p. 2.

7. Austen-Leigh, Mary Augusta, p. 24.

8. Edward Hugessen Knatchbull-Hugessen, Lord Brabourne, p. xii.

14. Observations & Opinions on the Novels

1. Austen-Leigh, J. E., p. 116.

2. Le Faye, p. 275.

3. Austen, Jane, *Mansfield Park*, chapter 48.

4. Austen-Leigh, Mary Augusta, p. 4.

5. Austen-Leigh, J. E., p. 150.

6. Ibid., p. 151.

APPENDIX 1:
THE AUSTEN FAMILY AFTER 1817
(in chronological order of birth)

Mrs Austen

After Jane's death Mrs Austen wrote to her granddaughter, saying, 'I am certainly in a good deal of affliction but trust God will support me.'

Mrs Austen survived Jane by ten years. She lived for the remainder of her life in Chawton Cottage with Cassandra and Martha Lloyd, who cared for her as she got older. Edward Austen-Leigh remembered that his grandmother was in continual pain in her final years, but that she bore it with patience and cheerfulness. On one occasion she said to him, 'Ah, my dear, you find me just where you left me – on the sofa. I sometimes think that God Almighty must have forgotten about me, but I dare say He will come for me in His own good time.'

Mrs Austen died on 18 January 1827, at the age of eighty-seven. She is buried in the churchyard of St Nicholas church in Chawton.

James Austen

James, who had suffered from digestive problems for some time, was too unwell to attend Jane's funeral. His son Edward was sent to represent him. A poem written by James lamenting the early death of his sister included the lines, 'But to her family alone/ Her real, genuine worth was known.'

James survived Jane by only two and a half years. He died on 13 December 1819, at the age of fifty-four, and is buried in a corner of the churchyard of St Nicholas church, Steventon. There is a commemorative tablet to James in the church, which is inscribed with a tribute by his son.

Mary Austen died at Speen in Berkshire in 1843 and is buried beside her husband.

George Austen

George was cared for outside his family for the rest of his life. When Mrs Austen died in 1827, she left the proceeds of some annuities she owned to be shared between her children Cassandra, Edward, Henry, Frank and Charles. Edward gave his share to his brother George.

George died at Monk Sherborne, Hampshire on 17 January 1838, aged seventy-two. He is buried there in the churchyard of All Saints church in an unmarked grave.

Edward Austen-Knight

Edward lived at Godmersham House for the remainder of his life. He survived Jane by thirty-five years. He finally settled the lawsuit over his inheritance in 1818, paying the other party £15,000.

Edward's eldest son inherited his Hampshire estates on his marriage in 1828. Edward died peacefully in his sleep on 19 November 1852, aged eighty-five. His family thought this a fitting end for a man who was 'an image of Gentleness and quiet Cheerfulness of no ordinary degree'. Edward is buried in the Knight family vault in Godmersham church, beside his wife. On his monument he is described as 'a merciful man, whose righteousness shall not be forgotten'.

Henry Austen

Following Jane's death Henry acted as her literary executor. He remained as curate of Chawton, where he acquired a reputation as an earnest evangelical preacher, for three more years. During this time he also served for five months as chaplain to the British Embassy in Berlin.

In 1820 Henry married Eleanor Jackson, the niece of the rector of Chawton. In the same year he succeeded his brother as rector of Steventon. He also, at some point, became domestic chaplain to the Duke of Northumberland and the Earl of Morley.

Henry later became curate of Farnham in Surrey, a master at Farnham Grammar School, and the perpetual curate of Bentley in Hampshire. He eventually resigned from the church and lived for a while in France.

Henry died at Tunbridge Wells in Kent on 12 March 1850, at the age of seventy-eight. He is buried at Woodbury Park Cemetery in Tunbridge Wells.

Cassandra Austen

Cassandra survived Jane by twenty-eight years. She lived in Chawton Cottage for the rest of her life, the last seventeen years of which she lived alone. Cassandra occupied herself with needlework and gardening, and teaching girls in her village to read and sew. A great niece, who saw Cassandra towards the end of her life, described her as 'a pale, dark-eyed old lady, with a high arched nose and a kind smile, dressed in a long cloak and a large drawn bonnet, both made of black satin'.

Cassandra died at her brother Frank's home near Portsmouth on 22 March 1845, at the age of seventy-two. She is buried beside her mother in the graveyard of St Nicholas church, Chawton.

Francis Austen

Frank's wife Mary, the mother of his eleven children, died in

1823. Five years later he married his sisters' friend Martha Lloyd.

Frank's illustrious career in the Navy continued. He became a rear-admiral in 1830, a Knight Commander of the Bath in 1837, and a vice-admiral in the following year. In 1848 Frank was promoted to admiral and was posted to the North America and West Indies station. In 1862 he was promoted again to become Rear-Admiral and Vice-Admiral of the United Kingdom. Frank finished his career as Admiral of the Fleet.

Having survived all his siblings and his second wife, Frank died on 10 August 1865, at the age of ninety-one. His family declined the honour of a naval funeral and he was buried in the churchyard of Wymering church, Sussex.

Charles Austen

In 1820 Charles married Harriet Palmer, the sister of his first wife Frances, who had cared for his daughters after their mother's death. Charles and Harriet had three sons and a daughter.

Charles returned to sea in 1826 on the *Aurora,* and was actively engaged in combating the slave trade. In 1838 he was involved in the Anglo–French campaign against Egypt. Charles was later made a Companion of the Order of the Bath for his part in the bombardment of Acre in the Mediterranean. His final promotion was to the position of commander-in-chief in the East Indies.

Charles died of cholera on board HMS *Pluto* off Prome, Burma, on 6 October 1852. He was seventy-three. Charles was buried at Trimcomalee, Ceylon.

Fanny Knight

In 1820 Fanny married, as his second wife, Sir Edward Knatchbull of Mersham-le-Hatch in Kent. He was the MP for Kent for twenty-six years. Fanny and her husband had nine children.

Later in life, when Fanny had an important position in Victorian society as the wife of a politician, she became embarrassed about the humble origins of her Austen forebears. When asked by her cousin Edward for her memories of Jane to include in his biography, Fanny was not very forthcoming. Her contribution was a scribbled paragraph, in which she unkindly described Jane as 'not so refined as she ought to have been from her talent', and said that both aunts 'were brought up in the most complete ignorance of the world and its ways'. She claimed that if it had not been for her father's marriage and the kindness of his adoptive mother, they would have been 'very much below par as to good Society and its ways'.

After her husband's death Fanny kept herself busy with charity work. She was also a devoted grandmother. She died on Boxing Day 1882, at the age of eighty-eight. She is buried in the chapel of the church of St Peter and St Paul, Lymsted, Kent, where there is a stained glass window dedicated to her memory.

Anna Lefroy

Anna gave up writing novels after Jane's death, because it reminded her too painfully of her great loss.

In 1818 Anna moved to the village of Lasham, between Alton and Basingstoke, when her husband accepted a curacy there. The following year Ben Lefroy was appointed curate of Compton in Surrey, and they moved again. In 1823 Ben succeeded his brother as rector of Ashe, and the family moved back to Hampshire. When her husband died in 1829, Anna had to vacate the rectory and move with her seven children to her brother-in-law's home near Basingstoke. Her life became a hard struggle against poverty and ill health.

Anna helped Edward to gather material for his biography of Jane, and contributed a short memoir of her own. She died a few years later in 1872.

Edward Austen-Leigh

After being awarded his degree at Oxford University in 1820, Edward was ordained. He became curate of Newtown, a village in Berkshire. In 1823 he married Emma Smith and was appointed curate of Tring in Hertfordshire. Edward and Emma had ten children.

Following the death of his great-aunt Jane Leigh-Perrot in 1836, Edward inherited Scarlets, her Berkshire estate, and added the name Leigh to his own. In 1852 Edward became vicar of Bray, near Maidenhead, and in 1863 he sold the estate he had inherited.

Edward had long ago given up writing novels, but he became an author in 1864 when his book *Recollections of the Vine Hunt* was published. In the spring of 1869 Edward began to collect material for his biography of his aunt, which was published at the end of that year. He lived at Bray until his death in 1874.

Caroline Austen

After her father's death in 1819, Caroline and her mother moved out of Steventon Rectory. They lived for a while with a friend in Bath and then moved to Newtown in Berkshire, to live with Edward. After he inherited the Leigh estate, Edward paid his mother and sister a generous allowance which enabled them to move into a comfortable house in Speen, Berkshire.

Caroline gave up writing novels after her aunt died, and spent much of her time doing needlework. She never married but, like Jane, acquired numerous nephews and nieces. Caroline helped her brother to find material for his biography of their aunt, and wrote a memoir of her own for him to include. Towards the end of her life Caroline moved to Sussex to keep house for two unmarried nephews. She died in 1880.

APPENDIX 2:
WORDS OF WISDOM

Jane Austen's novels and letters contain many profound truths about life. As the following selection shows, these words of wisdom are as relevant today as when they were written. Jane's understanding of the human condition is an important part of her enduring appeal as a writer.

'An agreeable manner may set off handsome features, but can never alter plain ones.' *Persuasion*

'An occasional memento of past folly, however painful, might not be without use.' *Northanger Abbey*

'Angry people are not always wise.' *Pride and Prejudice*

'Anything is to be preferred or endured rather than marrying without affection.' *Letter to Fanny Knight dated 18.11.1814*

'Business, you know, may bring you money, but friendship hardly ever does.' *Emma*

'But people themselves alter so much, that there is something new to be observed in them for ever.' *Pride and Prejudice*

'Distance is nothing, when one has a motive.' *Pride and Prejudice*

'Do not give way to useless alarm; though it is right to be prepared for the worst, there is no occasion to look on it as certain.' *Pride and Prejudice*

'Friendship is certainly the finest balm for the pangs of disappointed love.' *Northanger Abbey*

'From politics, it was an easy step to silence.' *Northanger Abbey*

'How quick come the reasons for approving what we like.' *Persuasion*

'Husbands and wives generally understand when opposition will be in vain.' *Persuasion*

'I am afraid that the pleasantness of an employment does not always evince its propriety.' *Sense and Sensibility*

'If a woman doubts as to whether she should accept a man or not, she certainly ought to refuse him.' *Emma*

'If things are going untowardly one month, they are sure to mend the next.' *Emma*

'I must learn to be content with being happier than I deserve.' *Pride and Prejudice*

'It is not every man's fate to marry the woman who loves him best.' *Emma*

'It isn't what we say or think that defines us, but what we do.' *Sense and Sensibility*

'Life seems but a quick succession of busy nothings.' *Mansfield Park*

'Money can only give happiness where there is nothing else to give it.' *Sense and Sensibility*

'My idea of good company is the company of clever, well-informed people, who have a great deal of conversation; that is what I call good company.' *Persuasion*

'Nobody minds having what is too good for them.' *Mansfield Park*

'Nothing can be compared to the misery of being bound without love, bound to one, and preferring another.' *Letter to Fanny Knight dated 30.11.1814*

'One half of the world cannot understand the pleasures of the other.' *Emma*

'Our pleasures in this world are always to be paid for.' *Northanger Abbey*

'Respect for right conduct is felt by everybody.' *Emma*

'Seldom, very seldom, does complete truth belong to any human disclosure, seldom can it happen that something is not a little disguised, or a little mistaken.' *Emma*

'Silly things do cease to be silly if they are done by sensible people in an impudent way.' *Emma*

'… that sanguine expectation of happiness which is happiness itself.' *Sense and Sensibility*

'The manoeuvres of selfishness and duplicity must ever be revolting.' *Persuasion*

'The more I see of the world, the more am I dissatisfied with it.' *Pride and Prejudice*

'There are people, who the more you do for them, the less they will do for themselves.' *Emma*

'There is a meanness in all the arts which ladies sometimes condescend to employ for captivation.' *Pride and Prejudice*

'There is a quickness of perception in some, a nicety in the discernment of character, a natural penetration, in short, which no experience in others can equal.' *Persuasion*

'There is a time for everything – a time for balls and plays, and a time for work.' *Northanger Abbey*

'There is, I believe, in every disposition a tendency to some particular evil, a natural defect, which not even the best education can overcome.' *Pride and Prejudice*

'There is nothing like staying at home, for real comfort.' *Emma*

'Think only of the past as its remembrance gives you pleasure.' *Pride and Prejudice*

'Time will explain.' *Persuasion*

'To be always firm must be to be often obstinate.' *Northanger Abbey*

'To fret over unavoidable evils, or augment them by anxiety, was no part of her disposition.' *Pride and Prejudice*

'Vanity working on a weak head, produces every sort of mischief.' *Emma*

'What a strange thing love is.' *Emma*

'What have wealth or grandeur to do with happiness?' *Sense and Sensibility*

'Where an opinion is general it is usually correct.' *Mansfield Park*

'Why did we wait for anything? – why not seize the pleasure at once?' *Emma*

'Wisdom is better than wit, and in the long run will certainly have the laugh on her side.' *Letter to Fanny Knight dated 18.11.1814*

APPENDIX 3:
PLACES TO VISIT

Assembly Rooms and Museum of Costume, Bennett Street, Bath
The Assembly Rooms, Ballroom, Card Room, Octagon Room and Tea Room are open to visitors. There is also a Museum of Costume which houses an internationally renowned collection of historic clothing and accessories. The building, which is owned by the National Trust, is leased to and managed by Bath and North East Somerset Council.

Jane Austen Centre, 40 Gay Street, Bath
The Jane Austen Centre in Bath houses an exhibition which explores Jane's life in Bath, her family, places of residence and Bath society. This is a privately owned visitor centre.

Jane Austen's House Museum, Chawton, Alton, Hants
Jane's last home houses this museum which tells the story of Jane and her family. The museum was established in 1947 and is owned and run by the Jane Austen Memorial Trust.

Chawton House Library, Chawton, Alton, Hants
Chawton Great House, which belonged to Jane's brother Edward, now houses the Chawton House Library. The library, which is a registered charity, contains a unique collection of books written by women between 1600 and 1830.

Winchester Cathedral
Jane's grave, memorial tablet and window are in the north aisle. There is a permanent exhibition about Jane and her life nearby.

BIBLIOGRAPHY

Unpublished Sources
Knatchbull, Lady (Fanny Knight), *Diaries 1804–1817*, Kent County Archives, U951 F24

Published Sources
Austen, Caroline, *My Aunt Jane Austen, A Memoir* (Jane Austen Memorial Trust, 1991).
Austen-Leigh, J. E., *A Memoir of Jane Austen and Other Family Recollections* (Oxford University Press, 2002).
Austen-Leigh, Mary Augusta, *Personal Aspects of Jane Austen* (Memphis: General Books, 2009).
Austen-Leigh, William and Richard Arthur, *Jane Austen, Her Life and Letters, A Family Record* (Memphis: General Books, 2010).
Austen-Leigh, W. and R. A. and Le Faye, Deirdre, *Jane Austen, A Family Record* (The British Library, 1989).
Edward Hugessen Knatchbull-Hugessen, Lord Brabourne (ed.), *Letters of Jane Austen* (Cambridge University Press, 2009).
Hill, Constance, *Jane Austen, Her Homes and Her Friends* (John Lane, The Bodley Head Ltd, 1923).

Holbert Tucker, George, *A History of Jane Austen's Family* (Sutton Publishing Ltd, 1998).

Lane, Maggie, *Jane Austen's Family Through Five Generations* (Robert Hale, 1992).

Le Faye, Deirdre (ed.), *Jane Austen's Letters* (Oxford University Press, 1995).

INDEX

Also available from Amberley Publishing

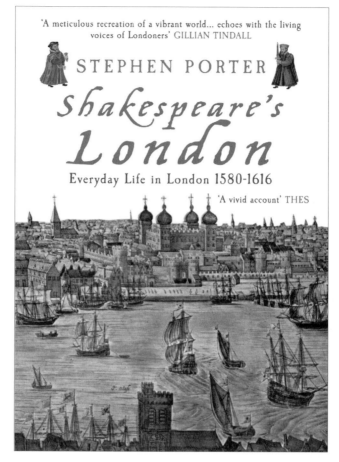

Everyday life in the teeming metropolis during William Shakespeare's time in the city (c. 1580-1616), the height of Queen Elizabeth I's reign

'A vivid account' THES

'A lucid and cogent narrative of everyday life' SHAKESPEARE BIRTHPLACE TRUST

Shakespeare's London was a bustling, teeming metropolis that was growing so rapidly that the government took repeated, and ineffectual, steps to curb its expansion. From contemporary letters, journals and diaries, a vivid picture emerges of this fascinating city, with its many opportunities and also its persistent problems.

£9.99 Paperback
127 illustrations (45 colour)
304 pages
978-1-84868-200-9

Available from all good bookshops or to order direct
Please call **01453-847-800**
www.amberleybooks.com

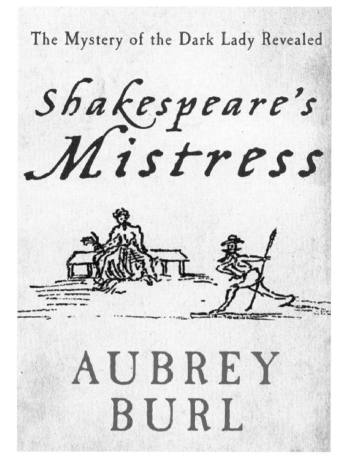